memoirs of a
MAD MAMMY

JOANNE HENRY

Dedication

I love a book that uses humour to tell heartfelt stories that can bring you to tears but also make you roar with laughter. My book is an Irish narrative memoir of my life so far as a mad mammy. I am sure you and future readers will laugh out loud and shed a tear at times when reading these stories – there is definitely a lot of emotion in every one.

This book is dedicated to our first-born, Jacob Henry. His 10th anniversary was this September 26th past. The date we will never forget – the date that changed us forever. We now view the world in a different light. I for sure have more empathy and understanding for others; I appreciate the little things having seen the fragility of life. Family to me is everything. He will always be entwined in the tapestry of our lives and live on through us.

I also want to give a shout out to my own mad mammy, Granny Ann, and my daddy, Granda Harry. Thanks to all my extended family and friends, your encouragement and support kept me going. My parents have always encouraged us to chase our dreams and with their encouragement and that of my hubby Lawrence, I have managed to stay relatively sane in chasing mine to compile this book. My sister, Laura, has helped me through gritted teeth to understand the computer world and to that I am forever grateful. I would still be fighting with cyberspace wondering where my writing had gone if it were not for her help.

I also want to say that I hope this book brings laughter and evokes memories for our rainbow baby, Hannah, and my hopefully-not-a-'plonker'-any-more stepson, Dylon, in the future. That he can share this with his son, our lovely grandson baby Ezra, in the future also. I know, I'm a mad granny now too and I love it. Loads of material for the second book…

Synopsis

'Mammyville', a word that I believe means a place where we all belong – we have all come from one – our beloved mammies. Sometimes in the story of our lives the ticking begins, the biological clock wraps tightly around us. In a fairytale ending it happens without a hitch and we live happily ever after with our bundle of joys. Alas, real life comes a knocking and it cannot be so easy. This book shares stories of the journey to get to the chosen place of 'Mammyville'. It shares the happy, sad and confusing times, all sprinkled with a dash of humour that I feel the Irish have in abundance. This humour, as you will see, becomes the superhero cape that helps bolster, guide and navigate a mad mammy through the minefields of 'Mammyville'.

This book would appeal not only to mammies with young children in the thick of parenthood, but it would also, through its humorous content, bring escapism to all ages as it helps ignite memories of childhood and family. It does not shy away from discussing taboo subjects surrounding pregnancy and fertility issues therefore helping educate and break down barriers, but again, done in a light yet heartfelt way.

It was roughly three or so years ago I started writing short stories about being a mad mammy, the journey it took to get here and the minefields it's brought since then. I began sharing on a blog through my social media site 'Mad Mammies' and the response I got were overwhelming. My American and Australian friends are especially enthusiastic in telling me that 'Americans and Australians love Irish stories, especially Irish mammy ones.' I suppose it is the modest Irish trait that we perhaps do not have a 'good enough' attitude or a 'Who does she think she is?' fear that makes me feel a bit embarrassed at attempting to publish my writing. I have decided to ignite the confident 'don't give a damn' and 'you only live once' attitudes now and chase my dreams. I have loved writing from a young age; it is free therapy for me. I also believe that I can help normalise the madness that can come with parenting in a humorous way by sharing my journey. Reviews so far talk of how my stories strike a chord with people and make them laugh and cry most of all. This made me think of a comment my old lecturer at university said to me once. She commented that she always liked to keep my assignment to last and read it by the fire. She said that I had a way with words that brought the matter to life. Also, the fact that she read it hearing my Irish accent made it even more enjoyable. She said I should write books. Now, that's not to say that the essays were always what she wanted in content (and I did have to rewrite a few) but the comment has always stuck in my head.

This is where I have decided to go for it and compile my memoirs into a book which I also believe would be lovely for my daughter and stepson to read and enjoy in the future when they are older. My dad, who is also one of my biggest fans, has always said 'go for it' throughout my life when I have confided in my madcap ideas. Again, those words were uttered and so here I go. On one hand, I like to think that they are wise enough not to let me try if they secretly think I have no chance – not like those poor critters on the singing shows who must have had their parents hear their voices and knowing they were not the voices of an angel they still let them go ahead onto national television. My hubby, on the other hand, thought it was a great idea and even better 'craic' (Irish slang for fun, not the drug. Just clarifying this for non-Irish readers) as he said he might get to go on The Late Late Show when I promote my book. He is perhaps a wee bit too enthusiastic, but sure – what Irish person doesn't aspire to go on The Late Late Show?

This book will share stories of the fun, happy, sad and heartfelt memories as a mad mammy. The scenic journey I travelled on to become a mammy and how tears of sadness turned to tears of healing and joy. I hope these stories will bring comfort to women and ignite hope for those who are on this scenic route as well. How humour becomes the superhero cape that glides us over many a minefield, which I feel the Irish especially have in abundance, which can shield us from other obstacles that may come our way.

This memoir explores how memories of my own childhood resurface as we travel this unique journey of becoming parents. How we reflect on our own parents, grandparents and of our childhood. To remember the joy, laughter and hidden gems that come rushing back from a scent, object or from seeing things through our mad superhero/princess eyes as (s)he discovers this crazy world we live in. I share stories of how holidays change when you become a mammy, but also the fun and importance of having breaks away alone without the kids. I hope that by reading these short stories it will help mammies all over realise that we all struggle with the minefields of 'Mammyville' and not to be too hard on ourselves as we are not alone. So, to reiterate, I hope you will understand how humour gets you through most obstacles.

I trust these stories will evoke memories of the reader's childhood and, for a short time, transport them back to their childhood or that of their children for a bit of escapism. You will be able to enjoy those memories, laugh out loud and remember that so often we get caught up in the rigid world of work, life and all its constraints and triviality, sometimes forgetting that the simple things are the ones that bring the most pleasure.

Contents

The Journey to Becoming a Mad Mammy and All its Minefields

I really should start with a wee biography of me, the mad mammy that I am. Who am I? That is the question I ponder a lot about. Well, in all honesty, I'm just an ordinary gal/woman entering her 40s who is coming to terms with being a grown-up, having a career and winging it daily at this being a mammy malarkey. In essence, this is what I believe qualifies me as a mad mammy.

Growing up, did I think that one day I would have 'x' amount of kiddies? To be honest, it was not at the forefront of my mind – not really. I did assume it would happen but not much thinking happened about the details back then. I sailed through my teenage years in a haze of carefree fun times mixed with the normal teenage angst years with the soundtrack of Lovers Around 11 (anyone from Derry will know this radio programme and identify with the ping of excitement of hearing your name in a love dedication or the tears on your pillow as you dreamed of the day that the guy you loved soooo much would send out his declaration of love across the airways. Yes I was and still am a bit dramatic, ha!)

My late teens/early twenties were spent expanding my knowledge of the outside world and seeing the world that existed outside Derry. I remember the shock and amazement of my friend, Marie-Ann, and myself as we made our road trip into the university world on the Harkin car journey of our coming of age. How, as we entered the multicultural land that was Manchester, our mouths dropped involuntarily at the hustle and bustle of this big city compared too little ole Derry. The different smells of the Curry Mile, Chinatown when back home, we were more accustomed to the smell of bacon and cabbage or Doherty's sausages. How we couldn't wait to say our goodbyes to the parents but then the sudden fear mixed with excitement that we were now effectively adults in charge of our own person. After a few ciders and pound pint beers we were an 'ickle' bit scared but would never admit to begin with. Again, in those fun filled 'Studentville' days, there was never such a conversation about babies except how to prevent them. Our lives revolved round attempting to at least make university for most of the days or for the percentage of time allowed before we would be asked to leave. The priorities back then were juggling our social life, part-time bar job, enjoying the fun of the big, bad world, first loves and then the heartbreaks that inevitably happened. As we grew we realised that leaving university behind meant that sometimes it's not much fun being a grown-up. Doing the typical travel to America and work for a period including injuring my hands – now that is another story! I think I caused my own parents to become a mad mammy and mad daddy in that era with the worry of me heading on me lonesome to the Big Apple. This was before mobile phones and video calls so we relied on the trusty public phone and letter writing. I had a blast and met lovely peeps – you know who you are. Vivid memories of attempting to put the world to rights over a glass of vino/ Lambrini, an extension lead and the light of an IKEA lamp in our Manchester student house back garden solved many a dilemma of the heart and mind. Although, when you get your first pay cheque, meet your partner for life and with that you get the added bonus of a stepson in tow, then you suddenly start thinking why we are here? Blah blah.

When the 30th birthday celebrations end, that noise suddenly becomes the soundtrack to daily life. What sound is that? Yep, it's the biological clock ticking noise; the broody button has been pressed and you have no control. Suddenly, babies are everywhere; kids are now cute and squishy, not annoying and loud. That baby smell is intoxicating – when meeting friends' new babies you are secretly sniffing that scent and wanting one of your own.

The next chapter begins when we buy our first 'doer-up' (our term of endearment for our starter home that, fifteen years later we are still in. That's again another story for another time). I become a proper grown-up, get married, become a step mammy to the lovely Dylon, have a proper nurse job and now we wait patiently for the pitter-patter of tiny feet. The plan was that after our amazing trip around Australia for honeymoon we come back and have a baby next summer. That's how it happens, right? We grow up reading fairytales of how life goes: man meets woman, they get married, have kids and live happily ever after. Well, I'm glad some parts of that story have changed. Women are now allowed to work and are not just there as handmaiden to her hubby – that she can have it all, career and babies if she wishes.

It is here we enter the chapter that we don't like the pregnancy journey and the one that sees us having highs and lows, the high of that first positive test and then the sadness of early miscarriage. 'Don't worry' the doctors said, 'this is perfectly normal; your body's just getting ready'. And so you pick yourself up and keep hope alive. The next journey is full of complications during pregnancy as the word 'miscarriage' was threatening – a word we previously did not know existed was taking over our lives. We then hit the depths of despair when our precious baby Jacob arrives prematurely and does not survive. We are plunged into a dark, dark place and the innocence of pregnancy is also buried along with our precious baby. To say hello and goodbye to your firstborn in the same breath is beyond comprehension. From labour to silence is horrendous and to bury your first-born, incomprehensible. It impacts not only your life but a ripple effect goes out to your whole entire family.

I guess, on reflection, this is probably when I first became a mad mammy, literally. You see, no one teaches you about this possible chapter in life. Why? I guess it is just such an awful thing that the world doesn't want to acknowledge it. I suppose even today it is still considered a taboo subject. Do I think this is the wrong way? Hell, yeah – in order to help couples heal we definitely have to educate and make this not such a taboo subject. It happens. Did this experience change us? No doubt. We were left heart-broken and the ache that began on that day always remains for our son. It's not so loud but never leaves. Tiny footprints make the biggest imprints on your heart.

The next chapter we embarked on was dealing with our grief, feeling bereft and I was wondering Am I a mammy? How can I be a mammy when my baby is no longer with us?

Will I ever have a baby? Is it fair on my hubby? The fight for sanity was a hard one. It is hard on a relationship and it was a rollercoaster but we fought hard even when we didn't want to. We read books; well I read books, my dearest hubby only reads Top Gear magazines. No slight intended, we can't all be bookworms. We attended one support session, which was organised by the fantastic charitable organisation, Sands. They deserve credit for the incredible work that they do. It was all that we needed to ignite hope, plus they reassured us it was not through any fault of our own. In this group one guy said a phrase that made us laugh in the car after. He said that this experience could either bring you together or blow your relationship out of the water. After tears flowed in the meeting we sat in the car and my other half turned to me and repeated the statement back in a serious tone. We then both looked at each other and burst out laughing, tears rolling down our cheeks. Great, big belly laughs and in-between gulps we pledged to swim this damn river of grief and not let us be blown out of the water. That, I guess, was another mad mammy and daddy moment. That night our humour returned – the tool that got us through the crazy journey of pregnancy. Through another miscarriage a scary pregnancy and more bed rest, until finally we had weathered the crazy storm. Our rainbow was finally here in the form of Hannah (Hannah banana to family). Looking down at that mop of McGarvey hair and chubby face we all agreed the sorrow and heartbreak was worth it.

Eight-and-a-bit years on and the journey through 'Mammyville' still amazes and exhausts me in equal measures. The minefields of night feeds, 'Toddlerville' and its explosions, the joy of hearing the first word. (The not-so joy of hearing bad words and realising she may have heard them from me –

eek). This is why I decided to try writing. We all need to vent our frustrations. To be an amazing mad mammy we need to know we are doing our best and that there is no right blueprint for being one. If we cope by having the odd glass of gin or two after bedtime or we vent our anger and frustration out to our spouse in trying to juggle all we have to do so as not to scare the child, then that's pretty normal. If we do get out on a date night, a night away on our own then this is healthy and not to be guilt ridden. Happy mammy equals a happy child. We will also learn that when our children our left in the capable hands of their extended family, grandparents, especially Granny Ann in my case, they are very happy and chocolate filled. Entering this world of 'Mammyville' has indeed completed me; it is the jewel that I proudly show hung around my neck when Hannah was a baby. She was the extension of my arm as we held hands, or she was the arms wrapped round my leg when a tantrum took place. I am sure the future will of course continue to be full of minefields but I also know that hanging onto our humour will see us through it all – that and the odd glass of gin is required, especially through the dreaded teenage years. We have been through this with my stepson so we are prepared for a lot of turbulence, but hopefully the second time we will be more prepared and have the fridge stocked with wine or gin for the bad days!

A MOTHER'S LOVE IS A BLESSING

Mother's Day has been and gone. This got me thinking of all the important female role models present in my life. I have been blessed with not only my mum, aka fabulous Granny Ann, but also my godmother, Auntie Jean. From my grannies I have learned a lot of life lessons that have been passed on including those of Law's mum, the main Henry lady – Granny Margaret.

I will begin with my mum, the lovely Granny Ann as we refer to her. This is very apt as her grandkids, like her own children, are her world; you only have to go shopping with her and if she bangs into someone, nine times out of ten her grandchildren are mentioned more than her own children! Her grandchildren in turn adore her and have all grown up experiencing the corned beef sandwich (these sandwiches with a cuppa tea can solve all problems – fact!) They have a stash of books at her house that they have grown up with that they love to read with her. Seeing her interaction over the years it is evident how precious grandparents are in our children's lives. If these relationships didn't flourish it would only do a disservice to our children – the memories my siblings and I have of our grandparents still remain engraved in the fabric of our day-to-day beings. I also know that navigating through the madness of pregnancy and all its minefields would have been so much harder without my Granny Ann's guidance and support. For this I will always be grateful and this is why I love her more than she will ever know.

Growing up, our grannies were important members of the family. I think most grannies were, and especially Irish ones. It was not uncommon to know your friend's granny by name as you did their mum. Sure enough, they were always about and just as important a figure in the household as our mother was.

There could be no more two different people than my Granny Harkin and Granny McGarvey. Even when I lived in Manchester at university I always sent wee postcards to my Granny Harkin, as I was closest to her as, after Granda died, she spent her weekends rotating visits from my house to my Auntie Jean's. She was effectively my weekend roommate/ spider killer/card playing and TV companion to The Hit Man and Her. Yep, she was a night owl and loved that show as well as Cell Block H, snooker and one of the longest and loudest night prayers senders I know! They got so long that after she would finish I would send a quick prayer myself praying that no one she knew would die for a while, at least a month.

When she babysat for us she would regularly tell us stories about her friends and family using a big selection of photo cards she always kept in her handbag. It wasn't until we got older that we realised these photo cards where in fact memorial cards! She had loads of them and we used to love looking at them. Only an Irish granny would use memorial cards as photo stories and not think it weird.

My memory of Granny McGarvey from childhood was that she always had her face on and had fabulous hair that she would pile on top of her head. She was probably what we would now call a glam granny. She loved her bingo and her best friend Peggy lived down the street – she had as many kids as her – twelve! (I know, OMG!) I guess they were each other's support network of mad mammies back in the day. Granny Harkin rarely wore makeup unless she was going to a do (Derry slang for a wedding, christening or general night out). She herself hated bingo and always wore her wee housecoat over her clothes to keep them clean. She also always had a stash of chocolate by the side of her chair. Ferrero Rocher and Maltesers still remind me of her although for a different reason as she once choked on them. I know, not funny! She boycotted them from that day, a dirty look given if she ever spied a packet in our house – as if the poor Malteser did it on purpose.

Even though the two grannies were so different in appearance they both shared a lot of similarities. They both loved their children and husbands, well, most of the time, 'keeping it real' people. They both realised the importance of instilling good morals and raised, on the whole, well rounded individuals with a dash of madness that is inevitable with the McGarvey gene involved (we all know it's true!) They both raised their families in a time known as 'The Troubles' in Derry when it was tough and was at its height in those days. That in itself must be applauded as I am sure this caused them both mad mammy moments trying to let their children grow up, but also living with the fear that they may get involved in all of the madness and, God forbid, get hurt. My parents raised us to treat everyone the same irrelevant of their religion and affiliation and so, in turn, their parents obviously taught them well. Yes, you can have an opinion and a lot of things in life will not be fair but, really, we need to just try and become tolerant of our differences and get along in this crazy world. Well, we live in hope anyway.

Mother's Day, lovely as it is for most to feel appreciated, can also be very hard for people, those whose mothers have passed on; my own mother-in-law being one of them. It does make me feel sad that she was taken so early and didn't get to meet Hannah Margaret Henry. When Hannah asks how her full name came about she is always told that she's named after her Granny Margaret who lives in heaven. This is bittersweet to hear, as we love that she has grown up knowing who she is, but that it would be the sweeter if she were here to enjoy all her grandchildren. She was a main supporter and comforter to us in the crazy pregnancy journey. Although she is not here in person we still make sure her legacy and personality lives on. Hannah knows she loved bingo and that she loved The Wolf Tones although Hannah is not so fussed. Perhaps this genre of music will be a grower so we will keep revisiting as she grows. She loves to hear her daddy tell stories of when he was 'wee' and the mischief he got up to and what Granny Margaret did. You see, it is indeed true that those who pass on live on in the lips of the living. No more poignant than one day recently, Lawrence was helping Hannah draw pots for her homework. She had to draw a big pot, a middle-sized one and a small one. I remember the joy and touch of sadness when he re-told the story to me of how Hannah had piped up, 'Doesn't the big pot look like Granny Margaret's pot we have?' Law said he thought, 'How do you know it's Granny's pot?' and had madly thought that his mum was communicating with Hannah (aye, I think he has become more dramatic with my influence – eek!) He was somewhat disappointed and relieved when she informed him that when helping me to cook one day (yes, I do cook some days even though my hubby does the most because he loves to cook; I know he's a keeper for that!) I had told her the pot was Granny's.

Mothers who have recently lost a baby/child and women that yearn to be mammies but for numerous reasons it hasn't happened yet also find this day hard. I remember the utter sadness that enveloped me on the first Mother's Day after I lost my precious baby Jacob. I was at work thinking it would be a good distraction but it only compounded my loss. Why? Not only was I yearning to have been able to hold my baby in my arms on that day, but as I watched the day roll on, observing that the patients in my care had hardly any visitors, it all saddened me. I remember thinking all these mothers alone and their children on that one day a year have somewhat forgotten the importance of this individual who has given them the gift of life. I do think that this still happens and some forget how precious our mothers are until it's too late. I would urge you to change that if you are reading this and think Eek! That's me. For as the song goes, 'A mother's love is a blessing, no matter where you go; love her while you have her, for you'll miss her when she's gone'.

We all lead busy lives; kids, careers and partners all take up our time, but we should never forget that we would not be here if it wasn't for the main women, the nerve centre of all families, the glue that binds us, the peacekeeper. In fact, the real superhero princess in all our families are 'our mad mammies', so remember to wish your mammies a big happy Mother's Day. I feel that as you get older you so appreciate their existence, especially my mammy aka Granny Ann – you know you mean the world to us all and we love you to bits. To those missing that special person I hope that in time your tears of sadness will turn to tears of laughter as you recall tales of your precious superhero to your children on this special day and let their legacy live on through them.

Stay safe and look after each other. Mad mammies, in this crazy world it's all we have to hang onto. You don't have to be one yourself you know, as we have all come from one and am sure you ladies without kids through choice or not would agree we all have a few mad mammy friends, colleagues or neighbours. In this crazy world all us women have got to stick together and support each other, as you never know when a mini explosion will occur.

MAD MAMMY MEETS AMSTERDAM - MINIBREAKS AWAY

We once had an unexpected last-minute city break, child-free, to lovely Amsterdam. Hannah had a great few nights with her godmother, Auntie Laura, and a night with Granny Ann, so really, with the beauty of technology she never missed us at all. We were the crazy parents that after a day of sightseeing would eat and check in on our wee beauty through the magic of mobiles and Messenger video calls. Yup, we were the two 'eejits' going to all ends to find a bar with good Wi-Fi and then chatting excitedly to our 'mini me' about her day. After a hundred animated air kisses and virtual hugs later we settled down to well-earned beers and grown-up time. Family/parent time success achieved. You see, it is important for all mad mammies and daddies to have this time as it means we return refreshed, better slept and ready to return to the superhero/ princess world that is my world, with renewed enthusiasm and less involuntary ticks, as the stress has gone.

Firstly, Amsterdam. I have to say this was always a place I wanted to visit from learning as a young child the joy of books and the story that was Ann Frank. I remember reading this book as a twelve-year-old and being totally engrossed in this story of a girl my age and the madness that became her life under the regime of Hitler. How her family lived in hiding in an annexe at the back of her father's business and when their world changed beyond recognition the minute they stepped behind the wooden bookcase that was the entrance to their new lives.

When we arrived at the house and queued outside in a line that was small compared to reviews I had researched before (yes, I am a nerd and do research for my trips) I couldn't help but scan the crowd and people watch. In that line there were so many nationalities, some with their children around the same age that Ann would have been. They clutched their leaflets that explained the life of this family and, with the excited chatter of the crowd, you couldn't help but become quite excited yet feel emotional that what we were about to see, yes, was the reality of a book we all had read. But also, that this was a true story and that if these walls could talk, boy, would that be something you couldn't read in a book.

Yes, some may say that the house has changed a lot from how it was originally but, in my opinion, they have done it well. Yes, it is quite futuristic and metallic downstairs; the old warehouse part and the offices of the Franks' business on the next floor now hold video links explaining what was happening at the time of the family's hiding. It also showcases artefacts retrieved from the annexe such as Ann's diary, all so delicate and fragile; they would have to be displayed behind glass in order for them to be preserved. There are clips of Ann's friends that display her as a normal girl and sometimes bossy and hard to play with. This made me giggle as it further showed how she was a normal girl who was flawed and not a saint that was perfect in every way.

It is when you reach the secret bookcase and enter the annexe that this tour takes on new meaning. It was very surreal when you saw how small these rooms were and how eight people had to share this space for three years. From the diary extracts and quotes of the same displayed on the walls, they did indeed have rules that I am sure were hard to cope with. They had to speak in whispers during the day and not move about in case the workers in the warehouse below would hear them. Now, imagine trying to control your own children, pre-teens with raging hormones and strops, stumping about in this day and age, and then imagine doing it in a third of your house in blacked out rooms. They felt very claustrophobic at times during the tour, never mind on a 24/7 basis. Thought provoking indeed.

The thing that really tugged at my heart was when we passed a wall that had all the children's heights marked as the years passed, each with their name recorded. Now this, I am sure if you were to tour any house in any country today you would find this still. It highlighted to me that even in that crazy world they were living in their parents still attempted to carry on with normal life, do normal things that would occur as if they had not been in hiding. I know how my daughter loves to track her height and at the side of our fridge we have her height chart proudly displayed on an animal chart. It also struck me when viewing Ann and her sister's room (well, really like a corridor) how, even back then, kids still had the rituals of posters on their walls marking their territory. Extracts from the book show the joy they get in the simple activity of cutting out and putting posters on the wall when they receive glue and magazines as gifts from her dad's employees who risked their lives to feed and clothe them through their hiding. I am sure we all can relate to that – my own wall went through phases of New Kids on the Block, Boyz II Men, Bananarama and the Spice Girls with some lyrics of the songs printed so that I could practice learning them (yup, I did say I was a nerd). I also had random pictures of black and white pictures of good-looking guys from my magazines of Just Seventeen, My Guy, etc. To see the similarities from my life as a teen to Ann Frank's made me realise how lucky we were and how sad that they had to do this behind closed doors for so long. I also thought how hard for the mammies in that annexe. To try and keep the family together, to cook, clean and nurture in this environment must have indeed been a trial in itself. Especially as they were probably more privy to what was happening on the outside and fearing that they may become part of it every day.

It may be because I am from Derry and have the similarity that religion can cause such divides that this story resonated more. Although I do feel that this story indeed needed to be told, I am glad that years later a little part of their world is still there for the world to see and learn from. A lasting memory that I will take from that tour was a video clip of Ann's father talking about his daughter. He talked of how it took him a long time to read her diaries at first when he returned after the war and found them. He said that even though he had a good relationship with her that reading her thoughts he had to accept that he didn't really know her and that she had kept a lot in. He ended it by saying that this made him think 'do parents really know their children?' This to me as a parent made me think Wow! This was a man that spent three years in close proximity to his child and he had to admit that really he did not know the girl in the book. Scary but also so real as, no matter how close you feel you are to your children, it shows that there are indeed many recesses in their mind that if they don't wish for you to share it is hard to access and accept.

Another part of Amsterdam that I found intriguing was the red-light district. The tour of the secrets behind it was informative, thought provoking and also at times hilarious (sorry, but I have to be honest, we really do share the world with a lot of strange and wonderful people).

Before the tour I thought this was the area that was frequented by the stag doers, the dirty old businessmen, blah blah. To be fair, on our walks through it there was indeed that aspect of it but it was also scattered with ordinary couples like us (yes, we are relatively normal, ha!) that either had stumbled across the street accidentally (so they say, another ha!) or were intrigued by the things they had heard. After the tour and from reading some memoirs from the ladies it kind of put my view in a different light. We wandered around the area like awkward teenagers at times (well, I did, I think my other half not so – men!) I thought, surely these women and in some cases women/men and some ladies of a certain age really should have been sitting by a fire knitting, not standing up in get-up from an Ann Summers party suggestively posing (it seemed so wrong to me but yes, this world is weird and wonderful). I thought they were someone's daughters for one thing. When they arrived all squishy and pure this surely would not have been the wish they had for their precious child.

After the tour I thought, well, we have moved on and women really can be in charge of their bodies and if this is what they wish to do then who am I to judge? Some admitted they did this to make good money quickly while studying whereas other memoirs showed the shady side that still remains of being lured under false pretences and feeling they had no other option to stay. Although it does show that they are treated a lot better and looked after more.

A few facts that I found amusing was that the red light came about as apparently the red hue is supposed to be more flattering to the ladies' bodies and it originated in a time where it also concealed rashes and diseases that may have been picked up by the ladies in a time where safe sex was not practised. I bet a lot of ladies are now saying, "Hmm, maybe I should invest in a few red lights," admit that thought (obviously to make us feel better about our bodies as we ladies are never happy not to hide bad rashes! We are ladies now, not bad women. Ha! That could be read wrong if I didn't explain...) Also that Van Gogh, when he cut his ear off, had apparently 'gifted' it to one of these ladies in the district that he was fond of. Interesting fact when you look at his art next time. They also had a wall where they displayed some of the artefacts that clients left behind. Amongst the many were a pair of dentures, eek... an identity card with the gentleman's face in clear view (hope he doesn't decide to visit the museum with his wife in future, could be awkward!) The last part that made me laugh out loud was the confession wall where visitors were encouraged to divulge their secrets in a booth in writing and by having it displayed would help set them free (aye, right!) Some of the confessions made you laugh but are far too weird and explicit to share in writing. Let's just say as I said before, this world is full of weird and wonderful people whom I'm glad I don't share their thoughts with so openly on a regular basis.

On the whole I found Amsterdam lovely. Yes, it has its share of smoky coffee shops that you can't deny as the smell fills the streets at points and yes, the red-light district and the attraction of the stag/hen doers can make it look seedy at times.

In reality we found it a very friendly, relaxing place with beautiful streets that lined the many canals and lots of bikes and more bikes. I viewed many a true mad mammy who expertly manoeuvred her way around the cobbled streets and traffic with kids in seats at back and front and laden with shopping like a true professional. They also looked fabulous, not a hair out of place and some had heels on (sickening really, and I know when remarked on same that my other half was sniggering too much when I asked whether he could imagine me doing this) although I can't blame him as I would be a disaster on a bike alone without the added accessories of a child, shopping and traffic!

I came home thinking that parents and especially mad mammies exist universally that through the horrific times of The Holocaust, the mammies of the red-light district, the Ninja-style cycle mammies. They all have one thing in common that their children are their priority. That they would do anything in the face of great fear to protect them such as Ann Frank's family and I am sure there were more than just their family in hiding all over Amsterdam but, thanks to her diary, the world saw it through her eyes.

That no matter what we wish for our children's future that sometimes we have no say in how they end up. Be it through choice or by entrapment into a world such as the red-light district. Lastly, I am glad that my little chicken prefers the heat and relative safety of me driving behind the wheel of our trusty

'Vicky Fiesta' (yes, we name our car as do many of you! Admit it) to ferry her about – that as much as I looked on in awe and fear through shielded eyes at the mad mammy cyclists, I am very glad that this is not the preferred mode of transport in Ireland, for all our sakes.

Fairy Hysteria Has Enveloped the Henry Household

Now, if anyone had said to me that I would spend an hour on a computer totally transfixed with looking at fairy doors and tiny accessories for your skirting boards, I would have thought they needed help! Even more so that I would spend my hard-earned money filling my virtual basket with the stuff and become so excited when the packages began arriving at my parents' house. The idea of this was that we then planted them around the house when Hannah was asleep and awaited her excited shrieks when she found another accessory; just as good as Christmas for her and us? Well, OK for me but my other half will pretend not to be so transfixed (but I have seen him look at those accessories with just as much wonderment as Hannah and I).

How did this fairy hysteria come to my house? Well, for those who work in the health services you will agree that tearoom chats take on many disjointed and intertwined topics of conversation. They can range from discussing everyday normal family life, relationships to new medical procedures, bowel motions and then to films we had watched. From there to wound care, suicide, self-harming (yup, all discussed as we heartily dig into our breakfast, lunch or dinner. It does indeed take special people to work here, ha!) And the new topic that cropped up two weeks ago was fairy doors.

I became very interested as my colleague divulged all her information on her fairy doors and accessories that had her grandchildren so enthralled. A few wee clicks on the computer later and I too had become mesmerized by the 'teeny-weeny' milk bottles, washing lines, bikes and swings – I could go on and on. I drove home that night excited to tell my daughter and see her reaction about this fairy world.

I have said before that my child is what we fondly name our superhero princess as, since she was born till her present age of four-and-a-bit (sorry, but can't be bothered with accuracy here, actually a pet hate of mine. When I entered 'Mammyville' and would ask 'How old is your child?' I would get responses such as 'Eighteen months'. Just say 'One-and-a-half', or I even once got 'Twenty-six months'! Seriously... 'She is two-and-a-bit' is fine... Sorry, I digressed). Where was I? Oh yes, Hannah likes to embrace all toys – no gender separation in this house. She did go through a stage of only liking superheroes, especially Batman, Spider-Man and Captain America, well, actually all of them and not so fussed on the girly thing. Although, with the arrival of Frozen (yes, that film we all kind of liked too but after watching it several hundred times we are now not so fond of Let It Go. I am sure a lot are reading this and agreeing). Since starting big school and the influence of her bigger cousins she wants to be in their gang and has allowed Bratz dolls and Barbies to enter her superhero toy land.

In relation to the fairy doors I was slightly wary if she would like them or not. For this to be believable we brought in the big guns, our secret tool that Hannah obeys implicitly. Who is this, you may ponder? Could it be her daddy or me, her lovely mammy? Sorry to disappoint but, nope, this figure is Super-nanny. A made up character we introduced into our lives when Hannah was two and the bedtime routine suddenly became hard work. After an episode of the real Supernanny happened to be on (you know the one I mean, the English nanny that attempts to sort badly behaved kids out and cannot say 'acceptable' properly, always pronouncing it without the 'p' sound – drives me mad. I am probably the only one that had noticed). Anyway, when we saw the fear in Hannah as she watched her do her magic on the kids we hatched a mammy/daddy genius plan. I will say it was my idea but will share it with my hubby being the peacekeeper I am. From that night at approx 8pm Super-nanny rings our landline (really one of us ringing it from our mobiles! Not rocket science but it works) and Hannah rushes to bed so that she remains on the good list, etc. We added things on as the years and seasons went by.

With this in mind I broached the subject that Super-nanny had texted me telling all parents that magic fairies were looking to live in good children's homes and would she like them to live here? I hadn't even shown her a picture at this point and her face was transfixed which, after showing her pictures of the doors and accessories, she was captivated. This is where the doors become useful for parents. On research, yes, as I have said, I am a nerd and did research into fairy doors – well, a bit. It seems the craze that has begun to spread is great to help curb bad behaviour in kids; that if the kids are good the fairy leaves wee gifts and messages for them. It also can be used as a travel port for the tooth fairy that kids up and down the country and beyond leave their tooth out for at the door and, magically, it is gone by morning, replaced by a gift or money. It also helps with potty training and sleep (basically using fairies as bribery tools – genius, I know!)

It also seems to have a healing effect as well, especially if young children have experienced loss or separation. They are encouraged to write down their feelings and messages to their loved ones and are told the fairies would take the messages to them. This, I found as a nurse, very healthy and heart-warming as what a great way to help deal with grief and separation in young kids than to bring the magic of fairies to help heal their hearts. It also persuades them to put their sadness down on paper instead of keeping it all inside. The fairies often sent them back messages of comfort (of course, penned by their family so they are able to individualise the response and further make the magic believable and comforting).

In our house we have decided to use the fairies' arrivals as behaviour monitoring, well, bribery in disguise. Hannah is now versed in the routine that when the doors arrives, if she has been good the fairies leave messages and gifts, but not all the time (the latter often stressed a lot or could be a disaster) but also to promote better sleep hygiene… Basically, I need my bed back and Hannah has suddenly decided to begin waking early and worming her way into our bed like the silent Ninja she has become. I then end up spending half of my night abseiling off the side of my bed with one arm frozen, as the duvet is shared between baby Ninja and himself. I am sure a lot of parents out there get this scenario and why is it that it is the mammies that always fair the worst, hmm?

After reading this I dare you not to want to Google fairy

doors and become as mesmerized with this magical world as we are. In a world that is full of crazy minefields and where kids seem to be growing up too fast, I urge you to embrace this magical phenomena and let fairy dust explode into your lives. In turn, you will see the magic and delight on your kid's face – priceless indeed… Do it when your children's minds are innocent and open to absorb all the mystery and excitement that these little doors can bring. Why? Because it won't be long until this window (or door, pardon the pun) will disappear and the worlds of makeup, boys, girls, cars and fashion will occupy their minds. Ugh, that has suddenly made me feel sad that she will grow up and be scared for the future, especially the teenage years. Poor Granda Harry always said I caused him to be 'follicly' challenged (bald) in this era with my teenage madness. I, of course, would disagree.

At present we have had the fairies magically appear at the fencing in the living-room and Hannah's bedroom with some accessories for the impending fairy doors' arrival and with that the fairies themselves – eek!

Hannah is beyond excited and has spent ages playing with the accessories that have arrived so far. She has also introduced her superhero action figures as well as Barbies and Bratz dolls to the location of the fences and explained the impending eagerly awaited arrival of the magic fairies. Too sweet to watch and not get a twinge of excitement myself. Also, on a back to reality note, I hope that Amazon keep to their expected date of delivery or if might be a long week... Although I have thought of leaving wee notes in the interim to keep her going, letting her know the fairies are watching her and to keep being a good girl. Embrace the fairy doors people, I dare you!

FINE LINE BETWEEN SUPPORTIVE SPORTS PARENTS AND SCARY COMPETITIVE PARENTS

I am sitting in the car while my superhero princess runs about the pitch at Gaelic training. Good of the hubby to sign up to the Gaelic scheme when he's working and I'm off. Not that I really mind as she loves it and great for her to get a bit of fresh air now that the weather is improving. Well, we are in Ireland so I really mean that it is warmer rain with more sunshine in-between. Not that the kids notice, they don't seem to feel the cold. Got me thinking of my own childhood where you went out in all weathers and the memories of coming in and heating your frozen hands by the fire and thawing out your rosy cheeks and Rudolph-style nose in the winter months. In the summer you loved that you got to stay out later, and why is it that the summers always seemed to have been warmer and lasted forever when you were a kid? It made me think that yes, today's kids do have a lot more choice in activities which is a good thing although it does bring with it the not so great competitive parents gang that sometimes takes the joy out of all this choice.

Being a step mammy I remember attending a soccer tournament with Dylon when he was about six and being introduced to the soccer scary mammies/daddies. That kind of terrified me and made me laugh out loud all at the same time. They stood at the sidelines shouting orders to their five- and six-year-old kids as if we were involved in the World Cup. They would also be shouting at the referee and sending him flying looks that, if could cause harm, would have had him cremated and I am not joking. When you clapped in support of both teams you noticed the glares from this species as if you had betrayed national security! Yeah, I gave that gang a wide berth...

In my home town of Derry there is always the stereotype of the Feis mammies involved in Irish dancing. It can be very competitive and I remember my own memories of my short-lived Irish dancing career. I knew that Hannah would never be partaking in that activity, as I definitely did not fit into the mould of a Feis dancer in my youth or a Feis mammy. A close friend used to make us howl with laughter retelling her days as the child prodigy in this world and the hilarious anecdotes of her training regime. How her mum used to make her cycle on an exercise bike as part of fitness plan but in reality she was sitting on the floor pedalling the bike with her hands so her mum thought she was complying and secretly she was sitting eating chocolate! How her mum did indeed become a crazy Feis mammy caught up in the competitiveness of it all and, in hindsight, did admit that she became more obsessed with the winning than if her daughter was still enjoying it. That even though she loved it, it did make her realise that she did not want to re-enter that world when her own daughter arrived.

Now, don't get me wrong – not all Feis mammies are extreme, just 95% of them. The hubby definitely would be against joining this activity more due to the madness of the cost of dresses, wigs, pumps, etc. You would nearly spend the cost of a cheap run-around these days or mini family break when kitting your child out for a dance competition – madness in my eyes. It is a shame as it takes away the real pleasure and tradition that Irish dancing should be. We are all proud of the Riverdance sensation but I just wish that entering this activity did not hold constraints for kids that are perhaps really talented, but that the cost of following this path makes it unobtainable or puts parents under pressure to deliver. Wouldn't it be better if all this 'faff' was dropped and we just concentrated on the fabulous dancers and not their costumes? "Hey, what do I know?" I hear all the Feis mammies shout as they read this, so I will say that I am a lover not a fighter and please refrain from causing me harm if you see me soon as some of you are friends. This is just my opinion.

In reality, cost does come into a lot of the activities that our kids attend these days and I guess that's just how the world works now with kids not having as much freedom as we did to make their own adventures free of cost. I get that – as parents we are afraid for the safety of our kids if we do not know where they are 24/7.We are now more aware of scary stories of abductions and bad men/women (as my mammy would describe them) due to better global news reporting, etc. Although I also can't help but think it is a shame that they miss out on exploring their own area without restrictions like we did. Yet, I also have to admit that, with the growth in technology and arrival of PlayStations, tablets, etc, that perhaps if our kids still had the choice of exploring without restrictions or using these gadgets that they probably, if I'm being honest, would pick the Star Wars game and play virtually with their mates than build dens and climb trees with their actual real life friends.

I am sure that many from my neck of the woods and age bracket have memories of long walks out the back roads and teenage romances were you walked for miles holding hands. How the tarmac bubbled on the roads with the heat (imagine, it was hot back then in Derry). The adventures you had exploring the haunted houses, scaring yourself to death with the made up stories but still soaking it all in. The fear and excitement as we gathered daffodils from 'McCorkill's' fields, terrified in case we got caught and, when safely out with the daffodils as your trophy, you felt like war heroes coming home re-telling the adventure! The heart-racing fun of entering the barley field and playing for hours, always afraid that the farmer would come and shoot hot porridge at you if he saw you (I think this was an urban myth as I have never actually met anyone this has happened to). We used to spend hours making rafts from wood and rope and sailing it across small ponds, jumping over small ravines from each side of embankments – the utter joy when you made it across and laughter from your mates when you missed and ended up a drowned rat. Did we go home then? Hell, no, we played on and our clothes dried in. We didn't want to miss out on the 'craic' by heading home. Playing 'Padsy' in the good old square was a great memory, or rounders at the generator that seemed to last all day. Of course, we can't forget the swinging, round lampposts and sneaking out a cushion from your house to sit on for comfort. I used to be able to climb up with the rope expertly slung over my shoulder, no problem. Now I just get vertigo when I ascend steep stairs! I think bravery comes with youth and declines with age – shame really. We would spend hours swinging or jumping off walls beside the lamppost, madness when you think of it. I would have a heart attack if I saw Hannah attached to a rope swing on a lamppost jumping from a wall. Playing with bouncing balls up against garden sheds for hours, the square was a hive of activity from dawn till dusk. It seems sad when I still view the same square, empty for most of the time, probably replaced by computer games and virtual games.

Really, when I reflect on activities that children of today have (including my own) there are many positives for the current generation. They have a lot more interesting and varied activities, but on the negative side they are a lot more expensive, especially if you have a big family all wanting to do, say, Irish dancing or a sport that has financial add-ons throughout – not just starter payments. I guess restrictions still exist as to how many you can do comfortably.

My daughter loves her Gaelic and has learned to share and work as a team. She used to be fondly nicknamed 'Hannah the professional queue-jumper' by her coaches in the beginning. Although now she has learned she has to wait her turn to practice kicks (well, most of the time. I call it dedication to learn and improve rather than skipping). Oops… Does that make me a competitive sports mammy? She also attends dance class once a week and embraces her princess side. She loves to come home and, with tutu intact, proudly show off her routine that has been learned in class, sometimes adding her own bits that she thinks we don't notice, but she makes me giggle as I remember doing exactly the same with my parents when I was in my short-lived Irish dancing days.

I do think that all parents to some extent can't help but get involved in the excitement and be competitive to some extent when supporting their child's interests. Although, as I've explained, I do think that some take it too far and we have to remember it is better that we teach our kids to be good sportspersons than winning hungry minions that will, in turn, lead them into adulthood with that same attitude. Not good for our planet, I think. If you are one of those parents that shout at the ref or complain about the coaches, etc, remember this – most coaches, volunteers, etc, work as well; they have families but still choose to give some of their precious free time to help in these activities. I, in turn, think we should take our hats off to these guys and support them instead of knocking them down because perhaps the side has had few bad matches or that you feel your kid should be getting more match time. They have to be fair and let all kids get a chance. Even if you think your child is the next Wayne Rooney or Ronaldo, blah blah.

I know that, for me, being a working mammy is hard enough to juggle with home life than adding in a bit of volunteering too, although I also see that there is a niche for me and others that I could fill that would help all in my kids' activities. "What is it?" I hear you cry. The answer, my friends, is teabags and refreshments. Always in short supply but always warmly welcomed. If you are a bit of a Nigella you could bake, but as I am limited to the 'add an egg and water' variety, I will stick to shop bought from now on. We all know that a cuppa and piece of cake/biscuit can help make standing at the sidelines on a Sunday morning more bearable. It may also help boost the endorphins and calm the mad mammies and daddies so their overzealous shouting can stay at a calm and supportive level. Let's enjoy our kids' activities as a community and try to keep the crazy antics supporting to a minimum – after all, it's only a game and it's supposed to be FUN! Sometimes that can be forgotten.

The Letter That Makes You Itch – Eek!

This week the Henry household received a letter from school that I have always dreaded since entering 'Mammyville'. Can you guess what? Okay, I will disclose; it was the 'nit alert' letter, eugh... I shared this info with close friends for advice and to vent because we all need to keep sane. It was a group of these friends that said I should write about this so after thinking I thought, 'Really? Why not!' It is a minefield we have almost all experienced and as we enter 'Mammyville'. It is a strange feeling when you know you now are in charge of becoming the 'nit or lice explorer' whether you like the job role or not.

Now some may laugh and think Jeeze, you're a nurse; you deal with loads of bodily functions/wounds, blah blah. Yup, I hold my hands up and say that since entering the world of nursing (especially the elderly) I am now not only an expert with mental health issues but also a dab hand at identifying Bristol chart stools, a possible urinary tract infection by just smell and can cope with wound care without gagging (most of the time...) Even so, I still get the heebie-jeebies when I hear about the little head creatures and I immediately begin to itch all over... I bet as you read this you are probably itching too!

After being informed of said letter by my hubby when at work I came home to find a lovely nit comb and head lice cream on the counter to greet me. I know... such a romantic. Who needs flowers and wine to come home to after a 12hr shift, eh? Now, you may say, "That's very practical," which it is. Although when I probed him on the situation I got a blank expression (I am sure all you ladies know this look of your man. When you ask a reasonably sensible question on anything and you get that look – the 'huh' look – the one that wants you to either hug him or do him harm depending on how tired you are). You see, he had gone straight to step two without covering step one. Step one being the dreaded 'Nit explorer' stage. When I pointed this out to my beloved hubby he looked at me as if to say, "Um, sure, that's your job." Sorry, I obviously missed that mammy memo.

Men, aye they want to be known as protectors of monsters in the closet, of bad men/women, activators of 'stranger danger', policing of scary spiders and peacekeepers when Lord of the Fly scenarios occur in the playground/pitch/dance arena to their precious minions. However, when they have to face the prospect of identifying and, if affirmative, exterminating the head critters, they hand that baton to their wives/partners. This for sure shows what I have always thought – we are indeed the real superheroes in the family. Even though we may be shaking inside and gagging at the job in hand, we will do this – we will get through it.

My plan of action for the 'nit explorer' task went as follows: I got our superhero princess dressed in night attire. I placed a wee towel that, after the event went in the bin so it was not a good towel (as me mammy would say, ha!) all the time silently praying for no findings. I attempted to explain to Hannah that I was having a wee look at her hair to make sure it was growing. Thought this was a good ploy not to scare her. She looked at me and said, "Mammy, you're supposed to be looking for nits – the teacher said. Didn't you read the letter?" That was me told; in my day I don't remember the teachers explaining it so clearly. Hey, she wasn't even scared so I got on with the deed.

It is funny how actions, smells, etc, can trigger memories; for the minute I held that nit comb the memories came flowing. I could clearly visualise sitting in the bathroom on a chair about seven years old with Granny Ann using her big metal nit comb. She was a badass explorer – no nit if there stood a chance. I am sure many remember the metal nit combs. I also had clear memories of the smell if one of us had a nit. The shampoo was on all of us just in case there were eggs lurking, ready to take over the McGarvey manes. Granny Ann had a military operation going. We were all called to the bathroom doused with this fowl smelling shampoo that we had to endure overnight and then rinse off in the morning. I also remember the nit nurse that would call at high school and we would be lining up one by one having our hair explored by the nurse. I remember the time a girl came out and said cheerily, "Yep, I'm fine – she just told me to tell my mammy to get this shampoo that she has written down for me." The look in the group of those in the know about that shampoo, the slow and discreet movements to get away from said girl.

Well, I successfully completed the task with my minion and was happy to find no critters had taken residence there and, from what I could see as a novice 'Nit explorer', in my first expedition there were no eggs ready to hatch either. I must say that I did feel slightly smug that I had got through this minefield and secretly, away from Hannah's eyesight, did a victory dance with my nit comb held high as the tool of victory. Although I did realise that at this time the war was won easily and I didn't have to exterminate any critters, I basically had ensured my country in this case that Hannah's mane was free from any predators at this time. I am sure it would have been a lot scarier if I had found the beady eyes of the dreaded critters starring back at me from the nit comb. I also don't deny that I may have needed to call in the big guns on this, aka Granny Ann, if I had have needed a wingman to keep me on track.

Hannah coped well with this although was slightly disappointed and confused as to why they had not made a visit to her head. She asked, "Does that mean I have dirty hair then as they like clean hair?" Hard question to answer so I replied with, "Sure! Mammy got there first as I am a superhero so they ran off." She took this as an acceptable answer and that was that. The nerd in me became fascinated as to how I could protect my Hannah in the future or even minimise the outbreaks, as I am not silly or smug enough to think that not many childhoods pass without these critters breaking the barriers and having a short sit on kids' heads at some point.

I have discovered through talks with fellow mammies and friends, some in the teaching profession, who have to protect themselves as well from the critters because of the little minions they teach – a professional hazard that I'm glad I don't have to think about. Tea tree is a great preventative measure as is coconut as apparently these are not to the little nits' liking. I have always used tea tree shampoo, not knowing that it had this benefit, so I will continue to do this as well as alternate with coconut to cover all bases from now on. You can also just add a few drops of tea tree oil to your normal shampoo and it will do the same job. A weekly comb out is good practice, especially during school term. Using conditioner is also a good defence as it creates a sleek, slippery surface; not good terrain for the critters. No need to thank me for sharing as Margaret Fuller once said, "If you have knowledge, let others light their candles in it."

The last word I will say on this to all you novice mammies, teachers and adults that come faced with this fear: Stay brave, don't panic, go forth on your nit exploring expeditions with hope that you find nothing and then you can begin the preventative measures as stated above. If you are faced with an actual residence of these critters I hope your task is successful at exterminating them from the heads of your minions, yourself or spouse. That during this process you stay strong, have limited Tourette movements, shrieks of fear and are also limited or disguised if your child is present. I think that after this task is completed, with or without you calling in the big guns (this may be your mammy or fellow friend/relative as your wingman, no shame in this) that you deserve a medal or glass of wine for bravery! I'm sorry that I have probably caused you all to itch during and after reading this. Just keeping it real in crazy 'Mammyville' and letting you know you're not alone.

Mad Mammy on a Bike

At present I write this with a very tender gluteus maximus (in layman's terms: my buttocks!) The cause of this is my first ever spin class completed last night. Well, I say completed but really, endured would be a more appropriate description.

How I ended up there was one of my best mad mammy friends who told me 'you will love it; great for stress and they turn the lights off and have loud music'. In my mind, that was interpreted as a mammy night out without the 'faff' of having to get ready, thus a 'win-win'. I could go for a wee spin in the dark with lights and music and cycle the stress out of me and get fit.

We arrived at the place, entered the room and were greeted by a lovely lady dressed in her cycle gear and a welcoming smile. I assessed the room: about a dozen stationary bikes and twinkling lights covering the ceiling but not as visible yet as the lights were still on. I thought OK, this looks like fun. The instructor took me to my bike and helped get it to the right height, etc. She explained about the resistance knob that seemed to be important and told me to just get used to the bike and resistance and go at my own pace this first time. She asked me if I'd brought a towel, which I hadn't, so she told me not to worry and handed me a few sheets of hand roll. We waited for the rest of the group to arrive, placed my water bottle in the holder, sat on the bike copying my mate and acted like we were professionals ready to take on the Tour de France.

Then it started, we cycled comfortably, the music was pumping, the lights went out (although due to the clocks going forward it was not as dark as I would have liked) but the twinkly lights seemed to dance on the floor as if spurring you on. I was in 'the zone', emptying my head and thinking of nothing but the pedals. Then the dreaded shout of "up the resistance!" I did so, not knowing what was coming. Few more moments of pedalling and the nice lady who had welcomed us put on her 'scary teacher voice', shouting for everyone to stand up and we all conform. Well, everyone but me; I attempt to stand and pedal with the rest but it lasts about three nanoseconds and I fall back into my seat. My brain is now confused, the good and bad angels having an all-out war on my shoulders. "Give up! Why are you doing this madness?" shouts the bad angel. I am continuing to pedal while everyone around me are still cycling standing as if they were born that way (I feel like I need a hug from my mammy at this stage, I feel so useless like the fat kid at PE). I glance up at the instructor and she glares encouraging looks right back at me, as to say 'keep going'. I look away, ashamed and feel like I am failing her. I decide to concentrate on the twinkly lights on the floor although this time they don't seem to be spurring me on but twinkling in a laughing manner at my poor performance. I glance at my wingman (my fellow mad mammy) and shout out my failings with the standing. She spurs me on and says, "Try again" and we have a little giggle and I get back at it.

The next shout for resistance and I stand with all my might and last at least seven nanoseconds before I fall back into my seat. The nice angel on my shoulder seems to be saying, "See? You did better. Keep trying," although the bad angel can still be heard shouting, "Why are you doing this? You don't need to watch these people make you feel bad because you can't stand and cycle – leave! Leave!"

I look around while I continue to sit and cycle, mesmerized how the others of all ages and sizes seem to glide gracefully in their stand up position and I feel deflated. My memory wanders and I'm back in my youth cycling freely on my bike, up and down hills, sitting and standing, showing off to the side. I have friends on the back and I still master the stand and cycle. When did I lose this ability? I suddenly think I want that back and I am not dead yet. With this in mind I try and fight the thought that I wish this bike wasn't stationary so that I could escape out the door and veer into the nearest ditch to keep my dignity. I would love to suddenly become focused on mastering this skill.

The music is pumping and I pedal to the beat; as we are told to stand I give it my all and with all my effort I manage to stand for most of it, only sitting down exhausted seconds before the rest are told to. I fell exhilarated; I swig my water like a professional, ignoring the dribble that runs down my chin and wipe my brow with the sheets of hand towel. I have renewed hope, this inanimate object of a bike won't beat me and I am a mad mammy who juggles work, family and all minefields in-between, so this will NOT beat me. The adrenaline is pumping; I feel free and actually begin to enjoy myself. Just as I am mastering the resistance knob and the art of attempting to stand, it's over and part of me is very relieved yet another part is disappointed as I was only getting into the swing of it.

I dismount the bike in a very unladylike fashion and as we finish our stretches I, for the first time, look at the other people in my class in the eye and admit that I was the worst cyclist among us. I laugh to try and retain my dignity. What I get back is lovely encouraging words. How it took them a while to master standing and that it wasn't just me. This is so what I needed to hear and the instructor said that at least I tried, which was a good thing and that it does get easier. I leave with jelly legs but renewed hope for the next time.

My fellow mad mammy gives me a lift to my car and we laugh at the class and how, even though I did wish to leave within the first ten minutes that I did actually enjoy it. That it did beat the stress out of me and I drove home feeling exhausted, happy and sweaty. So, really, it felt like a great night out except no hangover the next morning. Plus, wearing comfy sports clothes were easier to take off than 'out-out' clothes. 'Out-out' clothes being an expression my twin brother, David, uses for his heading out gear to wear at nightclubs/pubs.

I would say to all if you want a wee change in your exercise regime, not only to keep fit but just to relieve stress and have a bit of 'me' time, check out spinning classes in your area. It really is fun once you get past the first ten minutes (you really do have thoughts of dismounting and kicking the bike). They even do early classes at 6am although I don't think I will ever make that class, no matter how motivated I feel before bed. This mad mammy loves her bed and, unless I have to go to work or there is a fire, that's the only time I will be out of bed at that time.

Music and Smells, the Tapestry of Life

No one can deny the magic that scents and sounds can evoke in an individual. It's as if a door is suddenly opened in your memory bank of times gone by, be they special people/occasions to you or not. It may bring back a certain time in your life and the memories flow as you go back to that moment to share the joy and sadness that the smell or music has resurfaced. For the last week or so I have randomly asked my friends and work colleagues what their favourite song or smell was or a song that reminded them of a memory, albeit good or bad. The result was hilarious and at times so refreshing. It was as if, before my eyes, they relived the memory, became animated when re-telling the story that it brought back to them and, for many, they replied that they hadn't thought of that time or person in a while. Other reactions were that they would spontaneously burst into the particular song, sometimes re-enacting the dance moves to go with it (very amusing) or excitedly describe what they used to wear when they had been heading to dances, clubs, raves, etc.

For me, music and smells definitely can create a time line of my life, what I was doing and with who is often recalled when I smell a certain scent or hear a song. I guess it wasn't until I started learning about reminiscence therapy and music therapy and attended a course on them that I saw how they benefit and help people living with dementia and how, through the course you saw how it really does strike a chord with everyone when you open that box and delve in.

This got me thinking of my own memories and the first real memory of a song that stuck in my mind (apart from the usual nursery rhymes we all learned from zero age) was a song that many moons ago was part of a talent show on a Saturday morning TV show with Phillip Schofield. Claire & Friends sang a song called It's 'Orrible Being in Love (Google it, I bet some will remember, too!) I still know all the words and remember dancing round the living-room to it; being around the same age as the singer pretending to be her (I have said I'm a bit dramatic).

The song by Feargal Sharkey, A Good Heart, reminds me of my primary five teacher by the same name. I think he told us a story that he was the singer's uncle. To this day I don't know if he was pulling our legs or not.

Calamine lotion reminds me of getting chicken pox with my twin at Easter. It brings back the memories of sharing the sofa with my twin, duvet round us, having control of the TV and being pampered by Granny Ann through our sickness.

The perfume, Samsara, automatically reminds me of one of my lovely friends who practically bathed in it, that I swear she sweated it out too. You know who you are. My teenage angst years have a haze of dewberry and white musk oils from The Body Shop, along with the Impulse favourite of the time.

This was accompanied by the advert for the same and the song that went with it was always a hit.

The Spaceman song by Babylon Sue comes to mind when I think of Impulse (bet this jogs your memory too). The song Take On Me by A-ha takes me back to my bedroom and dancing around with a hairbrush, as does the song Frankie by Sister Sledge when I am immediately transported back to Uncle Liam's garden shed and learning dance steps with my cousin and half of the kids on the street. My first real grown-up perfume was Sunflowers by Elizabeth Arden that my mum bought me and regularly did each Christmas for many years. I even wore it on my wedding day as it brought so much nostalgia back it seemed like the perfect choice. The brothers had their Brut 33 which, when I smell it, reminds me of their fights when my twin found out my younger brother was stealing his Brut. They then graduated to JOOP! and Cool Water. A waft of these smells takes me back to high school where I am sure the corridors must have reeked of the mixture of these fragrances.

Shania Twain's Still the One reminds me of a girly holiday in Cyrus where one of my best friends and I sang into water bottles at stupid o'clock on our hotel balcony. My beloved hubby (or Henry huff when he annoys me) always re-tells the story of having a rendition of Garth Brooks' song The River sung to him drunkenly by myself and the same best bud in our flat with a mop and floor brush as our mics. He should have run then but we mesmerized him with our voices (that's my story anyway). The River is an all-time favourite of mine; one that I sang in public many a time with the encouragement of my other half when he joined my life. It wasn't only until many years later that I realised

I can't really sing but I did it for his amusement when I was slightly inebriated. So, I apologise to those from Derry to Manchester, America, all over Ireland and the wee Irish pub in Crete that had to endure this (yes, I was delusional for quite a bit, ha!) I now only sing privately in the bath.

Bob Marley and the Wailers' Buffalo Soldier song takes me back to the Queen of Hearts pub in Manchester celebrating my 21st and dancing the night away. I received, amongst my presents, CDs of him and Celine Dion. I am a complicated lady. The latter reminds me of recovery from a broken heart. I again apologise to my housemates that endured that recovery music with me – eek.

Lots of songs and smells that my friends and family brought up were ones that reminded them of their parents. Smells of tobacco, Old Spice aftershave or cabbage and bacon seem to be the commoner smells. The aroma of kippers cooking always reminds me of my Granny Harkin, but even though we loved her we hated the smell that came with cooking kippers. The wings of a cooked chicken were always the only bit she took as well, so that will always remind us of her (I know – the wings! I must get my madness from her, ha!) The sound of The Wolf Tones always makes me smile as it reminds me of the first time I met the hubby's mammy. The main Henry lady loved her music. We got out of the car and were greeted with The Wolf Tones blasting at full volume from her house, with the windows wide open. I didn't quite know if I had been invited to a Republican rally or Sunday dinner. Entering the kitchen I remember being greeted by a smiling face holding a pot of spuds nearly as big as her. She was known for her large portions and my hubby always jests with my mammy on her portions being teeny compared to his mammy's. This music we have tried to pass on to Hannah to keep Granny Margaret's memory alive. To date she's not as big a fan as her granny was but we will re-visit when older.

Awaiting the results of our A Levels always comes flooding back to me when I hear Waterfalls by TLC. We did a camping trip to Buncrana and my friend's daddy, the lovely Terry, embraced our madness, left us there and helped put up our tent. The memories of chatting excitedly and nervously about our future, sharing alcoholic drinks legally and just enjoying life always makes me smile, as does Mariah Carey, the soundtrack to our road trips to Gweedore caravan park before university. The Grill (those from my home town would know is a disco in Letterkenny just outside Derry that was a popular spot at weekends) to party to the dance song Freedom by QFX, but also to the slow song by Garth Brooks, Unanswered Prayers. Equally, the songs on my dad's favourite list of The Lion Sleeps Tonight (you know the lyrics: 'In the jungle, the mighty jungle...') The Flying Pickets' '...ba da, ba da...' from Only You and Jennifer Rush's song The Power of Love all evoke painful memories of him blasting the tunes as he mowed the grass at stupid o'clock on Sunday mornings when we were lying recovering in our beds from our nights out. He also loved to place the hoover turned on outside our room, as a sign it was time to get up (bad tactics when you're the teenager, but now the ones stored in my memory bank for our kids). My twin once woke me up from my sleep! After a night out he drunkenly made me promise that if he dies before me he wants Mariah Carey's One Sweet Day played at his funeral. At the time I was not amused and told him to leave or we would be playing it sooner than he thinks. Now we always laugh when we recall this story (yup, he has the crazy gene and, more than me, the scary thing is that he still insists these wishes be carried out).

The soundtrack to Dawson's Creek always takes me back to my working holiday in Wildwood, New Jersey, of lying sunbathing, relaxing on the house's roof terrace (sounds far more posh than what it was. Think rickety sun loungers covered by towels and mismatched furniture, but to us it was fabulous), dodging the crazy dragonflies that were like mini helicopters, reading and just enjoying life. The song Feels Like Home became a favourite of mine and went on to become my first dance song at our wedding. On that topic, will.i.am's Heartbreaker always reminds me of my hen weekend, jumping over our bags on the dance floor after one of my hens harassed the DJ to play this song over and over. The fun we had on that barge trip always makes me giggle – no one fell overboard and we didn't cause damage to the boat – bonus!

Staying on nostalgic music, we have dubbed the song Human by The Killers as our recovery song. It was on a holiday after losing our precious baby Jacob that this song came on. We had taken a well-needed break to distract us from his actual due date. Yes, it was a tough time and tears had flown, but one night amongst a resort where everyone seemed to have a walking aid (we didn't get that memo) we let happiness back in. We commanded the dance floor with the help of a little bit of vino and danced like no one was watching, laughed like we didn't care that our audience had to endure this horror and slept soundly that night for the first time in ages. When that song comes on we always smile and dance whether at home or in public – and we still don't care what we look like.

The song You Are My Sunshine was a song I sang whilst pregnant with Hannah. She used to kick like crazy, although that was perhaps attempting to tell me to quit singing, although I prefer to interpret it as applause. She is now four (nearly five as she is always keen to point out since she turned four, and of course I don't wish to elaborate on the actual months!) and still loves to hear this story and sings along with me now. She actually knows the correct words better than I do although I think that's a family tradition to make up our own words, a trait that my hubby hates, so I do it even more (boy, am I bad...)

Perhaps I have indulged a bit on this topic but I hope that this has made you think of your own favourite songs, smells and the memories and that when they resurfaced they made you smile. I hope they also made you feel nostalgic and, if tears fell, then I hope they not only made you a little sad if individuals have passed away, but also that the memories they evoked made you smile through your tears. I really do feel that memories are indeed the tapestry of life. I visualise it as a big patchwork blanket. Each square has a story with a smell and soundtrack running through our lives. This life we lead is full of minefields and rollercoasters. Yes, some shake us up and throw us sideways but we must always try and get up. That's what makes us unique. We all have our different blankets, coloured differently but oh so precious to us. Let's air that blanket from time to time and let the memories flow good and bad and then fold that blanket up and put it away till the next time. My blanket is now re-folded but I'm already making squares to add for the next airing. Air those blankets, people, and let the memories flow...

Heaven, Superheroes and Pink Princesses

Juggling work, home and husbands all takes its toll and then add the first drop of glorious sunshine we have had all week and all plans are quickly changed. It is Ireland so the spring-cleaning and general de-cluttering of the house is shelved in turn for a minimal clean, small washes, then off to enjoy the sun and play dates with alfresco dining on my days off. The hubby who, after weeks of being asked (he would say 'nag' but I would disagree of course...you all know that argument, ha!) has decided to power wash the decking and rid the winter cobwebs in time for our sporadic and unpredictable sunshine when it arrives. He, being a man, decided to praise his efforts halfway with a new BBQ. A woman would have waited till everything was all varnished and pretty to do that, but sure – typical man and his toys.

Lady Hannah is just so excited about her 5th birthday that isn't till the end of June but, as I mentioned before, as she has been excited about turning five since the day after her 4th birthday, it doesn't seem that long to wait now. The topics that have been whizzing away in her mind at present are very opposite in depth but altogether just as important and perplexing in her wee mind.

The first two of these topics are those of heaven and death. We have always explained to Hannah about her big brother that lives in heaven from when she was teeny, in ways that were healthy and not too scary. We thought we had covered this taboo. From the age of two we started the 'balloons releasing' party for Jacob on his anniversary at the beach and the last two years she has loved this. She runs heartily along the beach releasing the balloons and shouting to God to let them into heaven for Jacob, as it's his birthday. She blows kisses and we have visited the grave at Christmas and left small trees and snowmen for him and her granny, all of which she has done in a fun and healthy way and has never felt worried or anxious regarding heaven. She knows that he lives with her Granny Margaret that went to heaven before she was born and that they both look down on us all. Last summer on holiday she was playing in the park and we watched as she went and introduced herself to another child. The little girl told her she was called Margaret and Hannah replied in a matter-of-fact way, "Oh, that's a nice name. I have a Granny Margaret. She lives in heaven though," and off she skipped to play with her new friend. I nearly spit my coffee out at the innocence and humour in the exchange I had just witnessed.

Although, I would say on reflection, from her beginning school this year and learning how most of the kids in her class have two grannies and brothers and sisters, this has made her think more of her granny and brother Jacob in heaven. In the past few weeks she has had teary moments asking why God didn't let her Granny Margaret come and visit as she could then go to Northside shopping with her like she does with her Granny Ann. She also asks why her brother wasn't allowed to visit, as she would love to play with him. These are hard questions to hear and to try and explain although this is when the fairy door came in handy. We decided to let her write wee notes to Granny and Jacob via the fairies. She was so excited at this and enthralled when we told her that the fairies are allowed to carry messages to heaven, as they are special. A while later she arrived back with a picture of her standing with another child who she explains is her brother Jacob and she goes on to say that Granny Margaret is not in the picture as she in making dinner in her heaven house. I had to bite my lip from laughing out loud and having a tear fall at the sweetness of it. I explained that she knows she can't visit heaven and she looked at me as if to say 'Duh! Mammy' and replied, "I know; this is in my dreams." Silly me... With my help she wrote a wee letter saying she loved them both and many kisses were added. The letter was left at the post box of the fairy door.

Yes, our obsession, well maybe my obsession with all things fairy has meant the arrival of a 'tooty' red mailbox and a miniature floor brush to keep the door area clean. We then wrote a letter back (obviously pretending it was from the fairies). Hannah excitedly shared this post with us at 'stupid o'clock' in the morning when she spied it on her toilet trip in the night. She was beyond excited when we said to her that the fairies were told by Granny Margaret and Jacob that they loved watching her being so happy; that they didn't like to see her sad and they were well. They also told her that the brightest star in the sky at night was their window and that when she saw it to wave, as they would be waving back. This seemed to have done the job as she isn't tearful anymore and chats like she always does in a healthy way about heaven. She had also been chatting in the last week about how daddy is older than me that he will die first. In trying to reassure her that this will probably not be for a long, long time and that I will look after her always, she revealed that she was worried "as if Daddy goes to heaven first he has all the money..." Well, that made me laugh when I explained that Mammy had money too, she was much more content. Put a dent in Daddy's ego though, as he thought she loved him so much but that in reality it was his money she loved!

The next topic that has preoccupied my wee lady's mind may not be so deep but has been very troubling for her. This is the problem of sharing her love with all things superhero and then her love for the pink princess mini brigade friends. I will explain further: when she was smaller she could easily potter around in Spider-Man, Batman and whatever suit she chose and then be a fairy princess on the days she preferred this. Since starting 'the big school', this love of both is being challenged and causing Hannah to be torn between her love of superheroes and boys' toys and her friends that are, as I call them, the pink princess brigade. We have noticed that on a recent shopping trip she herself chose pink trainers and a pink coat and girly tops, well, with one exception of the teenage Ninja and Spider-Man one but, hey, it usually always is 95% superhero with a tinge of pink, so this is an anomaly.

Then my hubby noticed when he was leaving her to Granny Ann one day all dressed in her pink clobber. He said that her excitement at seeing her pink princess friends diminished when she suddenly became aware she was wearing her superhero watch. He said she discreetly took it off and handed it to him before skipping off with her friends in a wave of girly giggles. I think it was more a dagger to my hubby's heart, if he was honest, that his mini tomboy is now realising that all things pink are not evil. Although he need not have worried too much as a few days later her excitement at receiving a Spider-Man party invitation had her superhero madness return with gusto. She refused to wear the nice pink outfit, going instead for the Spider-Man top and red leggings as it was a "superhero party, Mammy, not a girls' one". Silly me again... She has also decided that when her bedroom is re-decorated she will have half of it in a superhero theme and the other in princess and pink. She said she is still deciding what kind of bed she wants although she definitely wants a bunk bed, one for friends to sleep-over or in case God gives her a baby brother and sister (eek, that's not so easy to explain but, hey, miracles do happen...)

Research says on the topic of death and heaven (yes, the nerd in me had to look this up) is that this is just one of the healthy phases that all kids go through as they attempt to understand this concept. Parents should attempt to explain it in simple and age-appropriate ways. From the ages of five to nine they become aware and ask more and we should be guided by their need to know, that we shouldn't bombard them with it all at once but add more as they grow so as not to scare them and cause unnecessary worry and anxiety. It is inevitable with the media that children are going to hear of death and tragedy more, so really we can only help ease their worries when they arise and so, for now, Hannah is happy that the fairies can communicate with heaven if needed and that is good enough for me. This was further reinforced that she was processing this in a healthy way when I overheard a conversation she had with her friend Jake when driving them home. He was chatting to her about his mammy's Granny Peg that had passed away recently and Hannah went on to explain that she will now be living in heaven with her brother Jacob and Granny Margaret. She also piped up that those we love that go to heaven live on in our heart. That was my input. It made me smile and want to cry at their innocence. Jake replied that his mammy would live on in his heart when she dies. That made his mammy and I laugh out and freak at the same time when I re-told this conversation later (we never want to leave our children; that is another blog on its own, mad mammies' anxieties regarding how they would cope!)

When I researched the superhero/princess debate I again found that when kids start school they sometimes do revert to peer pressure and tend to adapt to different social surroundings to fit in and not be picked on. That if girls do like stereotypical boy things that they will only really embrace that side when they are with their boyfriends or outside of school and be drawn to conform to what is deemed the 'norm' in the circle of friends she wishes to be accepted by. In Hannah's case she has currently decided to embrace her girly side. She loves the company of the princess brigade, although she also indulges her superhero side with her friend, Jake, and cousin, Shay. She also still loves to play Teenage Mutant Ninja Turtles in the playground with the boys and always wants to be Leonardo, her favourite.

Does it make me sad that I now realise Hannah is realising that this world is complicated with sadness, death, playground rules and that society also has rules and opinions that influence your decisions? I would say yes, it does in the way that it makes me acknowledge that she is growing up and that I want to freeze her (selfish, but true). Although it also makes me wonder of what is to become of this smart, inquisitive, funny and very clumsy gem of a wee girl (more trips to A&E is a cert). Although, what I do know is from now until then, this mammy will hold the hand of her superhero/princess as she journeys through the minefields of this crazy world. I will remain holding her hand through all those times (even the turbulent teenage years when I may have bad thoughts about her – perfectly normal apparently, I researched that too!) I will hold her hand and the tissues when she goes through heartache and disappointment as we all do in the journey to adulthood. Through the grace of God I will get to hold the tissue when she holds her dad's hand when he gives hers to her new man. The song from Mamma Mia! called Slipping Through My Fingers gets me every time now. I also hope that I get to experience the utter joy of holding her baby's hand and hold my daughter's as she enters mad mammy world and I become a mad granny (now, that will be an adventure).

Superhero Cruises/Relaxation Makes a Happy Anniversary

The weekend past marked the 8th anniversary of the day we became the 'married couple'. It is madness that those years seem to have gone in the blink of an eye. Seems like only yesterday I was fitting into my size ten gown (I still have the dress but would only cause me distress and the husband to much laughter if I attempted to try it on – that is why it remains in my mammy's house as I am sure with a vino or two in me he would convince me to try it on. Yes, he is bad and I would be that gullible with vino – I would comply). When I think back to our wedding day it brings back so many happy memories. I remember Daddy, as we were halfway down the aisle, asking me if he was on the correct side (I looked at him and said, 'I'm not sure but let's keep walking.') I remember the beautiful music that was a blessing as we had booked the singer blindly and quite close to the wedding date. I only wanted to know if she played Pachelbel's Canon and it was a deal (yes, even though I am known to be a drama queen I was quite laid-back in my preparations with some details). Thanks to one of my best mates, Sharon, who had married the summer before, she passed on loads of tips and we spent many a morning taking it in turns to entertain her new baby, my godson, Cian. We scrolled through eBay and, with a few clicks, had many a detail ticked on the list and at a bargain price too.

I loved my wedding day. I didn't have any drama or meltdowns before the chapel, which is surprising. It was more surprising for my dad and, in hindsight, I am glad as I didn't want to ruin the memories by craziness. Everyone seemed to enjoy the day; the dance floor was always filled (I had a fear of this not being the case and I don't know why). The drink flowed and there were no fights. Being an Irish wedding this is always a fear and a bonus when it doesn't happen, ha! I love that Lawrence's mammy was there and, even though we didn't want a video, we are so glad that my twin videoed bits as those memories we now treasure. That and the footage of my lovely stepson, Dylon, being all sweet and cute in his role as pageboy (we hope that when he comes through his yuck teenage phase that he, too, will appreciate these memories and share them with Hannah in the future). Even the memory of the fire alarm going off just as I was getting out of the shower the next morning still makes me giggle.

My vain hubby was more concerned about having time to put on his new clobber as we were ushered out, while I had to make do with my hair in a towel and wearing the hotel robe. I can still see the sniggers of the chefs and bar staff as we all stood in the fire evacuation point in the car park while I tried to make myself feel perfectly at ease in my dressing gown attire. Even my new hubby had distanced himself from me and was sniggering; yes, I did say he was bad.

Eight years on and I can say that yes, I am still totally and utterly in love with my hubby 5% of the time... and the other 95% of the time he is 'alright'. At times he can drive me to distraction by his easy-going manner, his 'half-a-job-Henry' attitude to DIY jobs and when he thinks he is always right. I can say this easily as I know that if you asked him he would probably say the same about me except that he would say I nag him about DIY jobs (obviously we know who is right but we also know who thinks he is right).

On our anniversary weekend this year I went on a cruise with Hannah as a surprise on the Saturday with one of my best mates, Sinead, and her sister with their kids. Now, before we embarked on this cruise I thought it would be a hell that we must endure as parents. The reality was quite the opposite. It was so organised that you couldn't even say it was organised chaos that can often be the case when kids' play is involved. The entertainers were fabulous and, considering the cruise lasted from 11.30am-ish till 6pm-ish, they stayed happy, enthusiastic and very interactive with the superhero minions – I was very impressed with how they coped (though I am sure sneaky coffee breaks helped them). The day seemed to whizz by and the kids danced with their superhero leaders aka Batman and Superman, with a minion thrown in. They had their faces painted by Supergirls and Superman made all sorts of balloon animals and guns. They watched a puppet show (that I kind of loved too), spent time in the soft play area and watched a kids' movie if they wished.

My fellow mad mammies and I were able to observe them from a good distance and also enjoy a coffee and a chat that, as we know, can be rare when kids are about. Between the three of us we managed to operate as one super-mammy. I had brought sandwiches and frozen drinks that had thawed out in time for thirsty kids and remained cold (I know – good tip I got from another mad mammy). The other two brought more sandwiches, biscuits, chocolate and sweets that kept them fuelled throughout the day. Hannah and the kids all enjoyed the day and there were only a few small, short-lived mini-meltdowns due to tiredness towards the end. I had a moment while the dancing played out and I realised that I was watching Superman, Batman, the minions and an army of tiny superheroes all strutting their stuff on the dance floor that I couldn't help but laugh and say out loud to my fellow mad mammies, "How did we get here? This is what we have become," while gesturing to the dancing superheroes. All we could do was laugh and the other parents in our vicinity also giggled as we shared this thought. The scary thing was that we really didn't mind, our kids had had a ball and we had enjoyed a chat too, so really it was a successful outing.

As we disembarked (and again, I sniggered as I observed the man in front carrying his kid's rucksack with baby wipes and his kid's toys sticking out of it. I am sure ten years ago he would never have envisaged this accessory) we agreed it was nice to escape into our kids 'world and the superheroes, princesses, etc, that this involves. Would I want to go on the cruise daily? Um, no... Was I glad when the day was over? Yes, and that I had successfully followed my mad mammy friend's car through Belfast and didn't get lost. Yes, this may seem hard to believe but my navigation skills are shocking. It once took me three hours to get from IKEA to Derry; two escorts back on the motorway from two lovely male taxi drivers – this is a true story; my poor Granny Ann was traumatised.

The weekend ended by us retreating to a fabulous hotel in the grounds of the ancient Castle Dargan near Sligo for a lovely kid-free break. I actually almost managed to read my book in its entirety on the journey down (obviously hubby was driving) and I am sure my reading helped us not to argue on the way down, bar one, regarding directions near the end (although as my hubby knows my history with directions I felt it was an unfair argument. From his facial expressions he, alas, did not agree. Yup, they seemed to say 'You are thick; all you had to do was read the directions I wrote out for you'. Yes, Lawrence, I can read your mind, ha!) Apart from that blip we managed a whole day relaxing, drinking and enjoying a fabulous dinner, which ended with me relaxing in a spa having a hot stone massage (that I call 'mammymazing'). It's like your body is totally re-charged. After you have adjusted your face to fit the 'hole' in the bed, you drift off and relax. It is the only time that I don't talk (and I love to chat – I inherited this from me mammy). To all of you out there, especially mammies – if you have not tried this do go and book it. I said it is fabulous and 'mammymazing'. Where did my hubby go when I was re-charging, I hear you wonder? He went for a run around the grounds and golf course. Each to their own and, as much as I love a wee run, at my hubby's pace I would have been running on my own, so my decision to relax in the spa was the right decision.

Today we even planted flowers together in our flower boxes on the decking – voluntarily – no one made us. At one point I looked across at my hubby and laughed saying, "You know this means we are real grown-ups now." My twin brother started gardening a few years back and oh, how I laughed at this vision, him lovingly potting his plants and arranging them so around his garden. He obviously became a grown-up before me! I now have joined his gang and sad to say I actually enjoyed it – quite relaxing. Will we be giving Alan Titchmarsh a run for his money? Probably not; if they survive the summer or until the end of June we'll be happy.

On the whole we had a lovely weekend anniversary. I loved that we now have Hannah to add a bit of crazy superhero cruise fun, although I also love Granny Ann more for keeping Hannah so that we could also relax in a kid-free environment and contemplate the next eight years together, eek. Marriage is hard work and I remember not so long ago waking up because of my hubby's snoring and looking at him in the moonlight with not a lot of love. Yup, I had bad thoughts and thought Eugh... do I have to stick his annoying habits forever? That moment changed, however, when he opened his eyes and smiled a stupid sleepy smile and, on seeing my not-so poker face, said, "You're not having nice thoughts about me, are you?" Oh, how we laughed as I honestly replied 'No'. Why did we laugh? Probably because he also has those thoughts over habits of mine he finds annoying and am sure everyone has if they're honest. Hey, that's OK. We are only human so I don't feel bad and nor should you, as I said, if 95% of the time you think your other half is 'alright', with the other 5% when you think you are truly, madly, deeply in love then I think that's grand. Don't you?

Daddies Are Really Superheroes in Disguise

What is a father? We may ponder on this question. The definition of 'father' is described as the male parent to a child. Now, really, if you were to think of your husband or own father I am sure that this definition, although true, would be much more embellished with attributes such as protector, provider, loving, funny and your own fan club kind of crazy guy (or perhaps that's just my dad). Although you would have to agree with the changing world we live in now, your daddy is really much more than the biological one. Some men, for numerous reasons, are not in the lives of the kids they helped create. We then have the creation of new families and step-dads emerge or granddads that take on the role of the father figure and are loved in return. I am sure as you read this you have that father figure in your mind, whether it is the biological or other. I am also sure as you think of the person that had this role in your life, that the lid is lifted and the memory bubbles flow of the good, the bad and the madness that is the relationship of daddy and daughter/son.

My memory bubbles are overflowing when I think of my dad, the main man, Mr McGarvey. Yes, I have to say that if Carlsberg did dads they would be hard pushed to replicate mine. We are very lucky that he is one of the good ones (maybe a hint of crazy but a good crazy and it's not his fault, it's in his genes; we all embrace it as we have all inherited it). Growing up he was strict but fair and always good fun. Fond memories of trips in our wee Renault always make me laugh out loud. The time my brother Harry threw a crisp packet out the window a big no-no! The car was brought to an emergency stop that near had us all in the driver's seat. My brother was marched out of the car to retrieve the crisp packet with a lecture on not littering, blah blah blah. Oh, how we all ended up laughing as he searched in deep concentration for the discarded crisp packet instead of just picking anyone to get it over with (I did say we all inherited a bit of crazy).

The holiday in Malin Head – that was hell for us as teenagers, stuck in a thatched cottage all sharing the same bedroom, with the memory of baby sister Laura peeing in a metal bucket through the night, always cracks us up (the toilets were outside and pitch dark, so not an option for a toddler). The song Crazy by Patsy Cline reminds us of our Auntie Theresa singing her heart out in the local pub and my teenage twin and I wishing to be anywhere but there amongst our embarrassing parents and family. I am sure everyone has a story where the dad explodes and shouts 'We are all on our holidays and going to have fun whether you like it or not!' This moment in our family, however, was all the more comical as it came when we were all crammed in a swan-shaped boat in Butlin's to placate the baby of family Laura. Yup, two teenagers, a twelve-year-old and a toddler being shouted at from the other swan boat by a near exploding raspberry-faced dad and poor Granny Ann by his side, wishing she was anywhere but there. Ahh, family holidays are the best.

My mum's dad died when we were still young and he was poorly for most of our memory of him, but mammy still told us stories of her dad and so, in a way, we got to know the man that raised her through these memories that she and our Granny Harkin loved to share. I remember Granny Harkin loved telling us how she met our Granddad Harkin, how she was five years older than him and so had fancied him from afar for years until he was old enough to go to the dances (and was probably legal to date by then, ha! Really, when I think about it now, she was probably a cougar in her day. Go, Granny, ha!) Daddy always winds mammy up by telling the story of our Granddad Harkin taking a turn on his new bike saying he was well capable and then crashing it down the hill...

My dad's daddy, Granda McGarvey, was a character. He was well known in town as the barber and worked in the hospital that I now work in and have heard many a story about his antics from people who knew him. He once told me that washing your hair with eggs was good. Not realising he meant you had to separate the egg yolk, I proceeded to crack whole eggs onto my hair. Suffice to say, after adding the hot water I had a plateful of scrambled egg in my hair that took me forever to wash out! My daddy would often tell us comical stories of his parenting that had us howling with laughter. The time we were fighting over bikes, my dad re-told the story of when him and his brother were doing the same, that Granda McGarvey had taken the bike from them, went to the back garden, sawed the bike in half and then handed a piece each to them and walked off, telling them they will not fight anymore over it (I did say that the crazy gene was inherited). He also said that once he threw a clock out the window at one of his sister's boyfriends as he had walked her home shouting, 'Do you know what time it is?' Eek!

When I met my other half, the one and only Mr Henry, his first line to me was, "Would you like to go for a drink sometime? I have a child who is in my life." Now this was as I was sitting at the bar nursing a 'hot toddy' as I had tonsillitis (yes, always a drama queen). My first thought was Wow, he is very cocky (he still disputes this, saying 'confident' not 'cocky', hmm...) Well, perhaps not but also that he is a daddy and he is letting me know straight up that his kid was important. Many years down the line he still remains cocky and definitely weird but is a fabulous dad even though we have had waves of teenage angst and rebellion from the teenager of the house. All part of the yucky parenting we have to let play out even though it is hard on the heart for sure. Teenage madness is like the acne of parenting. They arrive without warning or one by one; are sometimes stubborn and often flare up although, in time, they will hopefully leave and return to the state before the hormones arrive. He is a great dad to Hannah and she has him perfectly wrapped round her tiny finger. She thinks he is the best thing since sliced bread. He is the monster catcher, the pram fixer, the greatest curry maker, the man with all the money whom he gets to share it with her too much (although he would say she is not spoilt). He is, in her eyes, the bravest, and strongest and fixer of everything really – a superhero in disguise... and he is moving up a mountain when she hits the teenage years.

They say that daughters sometimes end up marrying someone who reminds them of their dad. I can visualise my dad and hubby now laughing and shouting out 'no way' as they read this. On reflection I can see why this can be said. My hubby and dad are opposite in some ways. My dad is a joiner and can put his hand to most things. My hubby can also put his hand to many things like DIY (although I have to nag him as I mentioned earlier), but then I have to get my dad's hands or his tradesmen friends to fix it (no Henry huffs, you know it's true, but you are fabulous at your job!) They are also, when I think of it, similar in many ways. They can both cook better than their wives (sorry mammy, but it's true). They both ran a marathon and I am sure my hubby is now shouting out, 'I ran five!' He is much more competitive. They also love Derry City FC. Most of all I can say they are great dads who love their kids even when their kids don't think they love them in their teenage years. The memory of Granda Harry removing my door for slamming it and carrying it down the stairs on his shoulder makes me laugh now, but at the time I wanted to emancipate myself from him for cruelty and deprivation of privacy (yes, I was an annoying teenager in my 16th year). They both have that crazy gene that makes you love them but also makes you want to shake them when they huff. They are both very good 'huffers' the two main men in my life, although as time has passed they do admit this and the duration of huffs have lessened.

I think as we grow older and, especially when you become parents yourself, you see your parents in a different light. They are always your parents whom you respect and look up to but they also become your friends and you actually spend time with them because you want to. They don't embarrass you like when you were younger (actually, that's not true, they both can still do that but that's OK as we accept it now). My hubby regularly went to Derry matches with his son and his dad and recently went to an Arsenal match with his dad that was lovely to see the pictures of them doing something fun together. Equally funny is the face he pulled when I told him that his mannerisms and the way he is becoming quite holy reminds me of his dad, but hey, no better man to be like.

Father's Day can be a very hard day for people who have lost their dads recently or who are no longer in their lives through no fault of their own. I know that as I have seen my friends' dads pass on; you feel that pain for them as you understand that this is a universal loss we all have to face one day and when that happens a big jigsaw piece will be missing from your family. To all that are finding this day hard I hope that when tears fall in time they will turn to tears of laughter as you reminisce of the great man in your life and re-tell your stories to your children and grandchildren so that his memory remains alive in your hearts. To those that are reading this and do not appreciate how precious your dads are, I hope you do now and spend time enjoying life and making time for family. We all lead busy, complicated lives and juggling all the balls can be hard, but don't get to the point where it's too late and regrets set in when you realise that an important part of your tapestry is gone and can never be replaced. Daddy figures rock whether they are biological/step/granddad. So enjoy your day, daddies of all denominations, and mammies/daughters persevere as they hog the TV with football, etc, as their day only comes once a year.

Holidays With Different Accessories as Life Changes

I write this with sporadic tics caused by the itching of four mosquito bites that I have returned from holidays with as souvenirs (unwanted, by the way) I had actually thought that I had escaped their clutches this time as it was not until the sixth night that I became their prey. Now my theory as to why they succeeded is that my inferior half took us for a meal at a place that was recommended by a barman. Even though it was yum it was located beside water and one of the hottest nights of the holidays ever. In my haste to get myself and Hannah ready (cause that's what mad mammies do, not only get ourselves ready but also the minions. 'Yup!' I hear ye yell!) I forgot to put on some of the anti-mosquito repellent that the taxi driver transferring us to the hotel had told me worked a treat. I was already hot and bothered before walking to the restaurant, causing me to be hotter (another factor that mosquitoes love, sweet sweat directing them to fresh bait). I know that from my research (yes, I research all, self-professing nerd as I have said before) it shows that, sometimes, no matter what preventative measures are taken you can sometimes can never escape their clutches. Also, that it can be due to your blood type that they are attracted to or the location of the restaurant being beside the water and on a very hot night, all factors that they thrive in. I was also wearing a leopard print dress and black crochet cardigan and apparently they are attracted to dark colours and you really should wear bright colours, especially at night. My research also showed that they like to feed on those who may not wash regularly and have stale sweat. They can also go for people with a larger body mass on them; this I know is not directed at me as I shower a lot especially on holiday and I am curvaceous, not overweight! This fact I am sure made the other half giggle too much! I also read that they don't like lavender and the dress I wore was new whereas the majority of my clothes have been washed in lavender softener so there might be something in that.

Apart from my fight with mosquitoes we did have a fabulous holiday. We stayed in a Spanish resort so it was lovely for a change being in the minority of English speaking guests and also made us attempt to converse badly, I may add, in the small Spanish sayings we found via Google. The staff obviously found it amusing but they loved that we tried. Hannah had great fun joining the kids' club with the encouragement of two staff who spoke English. She soon joined in despite the language barrier and loved the dancing and singing of Spanish songs. She also loved being a minion in the play even though she did fall asleep on stage at the end. The siesta nap is hard for Irish kids to do as Spanish kids are used to staying up late whereas Hannah couldn't handle it. Thank God for Daddy who carried her safely to bed.

A few observations I found whilst there was that Spanish, Danish and actually pretty much all Europeans have far too many beautiful people. I once had this conversation with another Irish friend and they agreed. She relayed that her husband had said that is why the Irish are famous for their humour so they can cope with being compared to burnt potatoes amongst the gloriously roasted Mediterranean-looking vegetables that are our fellow Europeans! They all seem to hold themselves so well even at the beach.

We went once with Hannah; it was a disaster. Our towels became covered in sand straight away. Hannah and I resembled sand doughnuts within seconds. Juice was spilled in five minutes and Hannah wanted to pee and complained the sand was too hot. I am sure that the two beautiful families at either side found us very amusing entertainment as observed from their perfectly straight, juice-free towels where they lay looking perfectly fabulous drinking in the rays of the sun. I, on the other hand, when Law had trundled off to find a loo with Hannah, attempted to clean the juice spillage up, not very glamorously though, and fix the towels that where doing a good attempt at becoming Aladdin's magic mat and near taking off with the wind that was a 'blowing. When I had finally anchored them down using bags and the Spider-Man swimming ring I attempted to lay my Irish body that showed off my love of food, well, in a not-so-scary fashion for others on the beach. After re-positioning my sand doughnut body I finally settled and secretly glanced side to side at the beautiful families through the safety of my sunglasses and felt a tiny bit smug that I was perhaps equal to their beach etiquette. That thought lasted just five more minutes when Hannah returned with an irate Irish-wielding daddy speaking very fast, barging about the toilets being locked, blah blah. So within a half hour of us arriving at the beach we packed up our soggy towels and took our sand-covered bodies back to the pool side.

The pool was a hit for Hannah with the child-friendly slides, etc; they kept her amused for hours. Here again I noted a difference in accessories with my Spanish and European counterparts. They carried their kids' swimming gear with such grace and some I observed had their big Louis Vuitton or Chanel bags slung perfectly over their shoulders – not a speckle of sweat between them in the mid-30s heat. Now I, on the other hand, used to arrive at sun beds with my bright yellow bag adorning smiley face logo and a 'We love shopping' message on the front (the bag that we had borrowed/stolen from Granny Ann). I usually had a Spider-Man swimming ring hanging off some limb and again, had my body that loves food covered in a nice swimsuit coverall that was purchased from the beach stalls. This made me at least feel a bit on par with my fellow Europeans as they all seemed to sport the same ones. It made me laugh as it reminded me of when Primark had a bargain top for sale in Derry and then you notice everyone has bought one too! Unlike their perfectly tamed luscious locks, mine resembled the Monica 'do 'from Friends when she went on holiday. Yes, I fuzz up at the mere mention of heat so a topknot helped to disguise that failing.

This got me thinking as I lay (with one eye while watching Hannah with the other) attempting to read my book that was purchased at the airport and, by end of holidays, resembled a dog-eared book that had been through the wars with spills, etc. Really, it looked like it had partied Ibiza-style when we had slept. I reminisced of holidays pre-Hannah of how we had cheap holidays where we didn't really mind what the accommodation was like as long as they were clean as we spent most of the time out exploring and partying by night. That even though I was thinner, especially on my honeymoon (the thinnest I ever was) I was never confident in a bikini and wanted something changed about it. Oh, how I wish I could talk to that girl now and tell her to 'wise up as your body will be worse post-Hannah, so enjoy'.

This, I noted, is another reason how we differ from our European friends. Yes, a lot look fabulous even after kids (sickening really, but blaming their good genes makes me feel better!) I also observed many European mad mammies that had all the shapes of 'I love my food'/post-baby bodies but carried themselves so confidently that they looked fabulous. This, I think, is what the Irish lack, being confident when we in are swimwear. I guess the fact that 350 days of the year we cover up is a reason we fail, as our weather does not give us enough practice. The actual swimwear costume I now feel better post-Hannah in is a halter neck all in one suit as opposed to bikinis. Kids have a tendency to grab you and jump all over you and I couldn't cope with an accidental breast exposure – that would for sure cause great anxiety to the Irish Catholic etiquette in me.

I noticed my fellow European mammies wore an array of styles: some skimpy, some all in one and all with kids hanging off them like stylish jewels – not like Hannah when she jumped on me in superhero moves and I resembled a crazed flailing Irish woman gasping for breath (this is especially true when exiting the tunnel slides where, as the Spanish mammy had her sleek ponytail intact on exiting with her kid and I was fighting through my hair to breathe! This holiday I embraced their confidence and enjoyed the pool and my time acting as an 'eejit' with Hannah and less time on worrying about how

I looked (of course I breathed in when exiting pool and my towel was on me like a protective armour in nanoseconds, I can't change the habit of a lifetime in one week) but I have to say I let my Monica-style hair flow and made sure I had my factor 50 protecting my Celtic skin, that of my hubby and Hannah. We had a ball by the pool and didn't return to the beach for all our sanity...

Food, glorious food is my hubby's favourite topic (from when he has finished breakfast it is never long before I receive a text if at work or a question asking 'What's for dinner?' Am I the only one who has a hubby like this?) Before Hannah we never did all-inclusive holidays and just ate out, usually tasting the local cuisine and really, the beers and alcohol of that region. Oh, how that has changed since Lady Hannah arrived and with our dearly beloved estranged teenager, Dylon, as long as burgers are on the menu and chips he is happy. We mostly holidayed at home when he was small as we didn't have as much disposable income as I was training as a nurse, we had just bought our starter home (that we are still in – running joke) and the hubby also hated flying and wouldn't fly until a year before our wedding.

Dylon had a foreign holiday when was a pre-teen with his mammy which he hated and moaned about – the heat, the food, etc, so much that his mum vowed never to go abroad again until he was older. He never wanted to go either until he was fifteen. With monetary bribery and new sports clobber we persuaded him to go to Euro Disney with Hannah, which he loved but will always deny. Since Hannah has arrived and Dylon no longer thinks holidays with the family or us ourselves at the minute are cool, things have changed. We believe all-inclusive holidays are the way to go. It keeps Hannah hydrated and our money is not drained as she drinks a lot in the heat. She loves the soups and bread and usually most of the chicken and meat dishes, always with a sprinkle of chips.

The hotel we stayed at this time had delicious food. The fresh breads and desserts were too good and I think I have now become more curvaceous due to the same. Hannah and I used to find it amusing watching Daddy Henry attack the buffet like it was Supermarket Sweep. I swear his eyes glazed over trying to take all the dishes in at once and I am sure his pace was what I usually run at as he circled the aisles more than once at each sitting, just to make sure he didn't miss any new dishes. This was another thing that puzzled me – how our European counterparts consume so much bread, cheese and wine and still remain fabulous (it has to be in their genetic makeup). Yes, we did consume some local beer and wine (we were on holidays but unlike pre-Hannah holidays we walked straight to at the end of the night to rooms not taking in each side of corridor – pre-kids' holidays, ha!) Hannah was our bedtime alarm and wake up alarm although she did sleep later there than here. I think that was due to her one hundred turns on the slide exhausting her out!

So, my advice for family holidays is definitely to purchase roll-on anti-mosquito deodorant or repellent, especially if you are prone to being bitten – bracelets for the kids worked for Hannah. Never let your hubby convince you to dine near the water when very hot, if unprotected. Launder your clothes in lavender, wear bright clothes at night and, if you still get bitten, it's probably due to your blood type and sweet blood, not because you're a sweaty, non-showering larger person! The all inclusive option is good for all as food is important when you are not consuming as much alcohol as you did pre-kids holidays. Don't let your lack of swimsuit confidence spoil your time with the kids. They are only small for a short time and they don't care what size their mammy is. Factor 50 is good for Celtic skin and wetsuit-style costumes for the kids. They are in the pool so much that without protection, especially with our skin, kids get sunburned even though they are wearing sunscreen.

Oh, and always remember to lift your kids' teddies out of bed in the morning. We narrowly escaped a tragedy when two of Hannah's teddies went missing that had been wrapped up in sheets when Hannah was playing. Thank goodness her beloved George was on top of the dresser. Daddy Henry had to make a midnight dash to the stall to retrieve another 'Leo', the tortoise and we had to make up a story that 'Peppa' had flown home to tidy the house and order pizza for our return. We then had to make an emergency stop on the way home to purchase a new 'Peppa' as Hannah slept. Daddy then placed it by the fairy door with a note letting Hannah know that she got in through the fairies' door and a secret call to the pizza place was made – Hannah was convinced of it all. We were both relieved and exhausted, so to prevent this happening to you, remember to keep teddies out of their bedding.

Holidays are definitely good for the soul no matter whether it is camping in the rain (we have fond memories of Achill Island when Dylon was young; he loved it so much stayed an extra rainy day) or sun holidays (also fun – it really depends on your preference and budget) although, really, no matter what you do it's about enjoying the simple things with the ones you love without the stresses of work, etc. It enables us to re-charge, make memories and to really appreciate our family before we return to juggling the life of a mad mammy and dreaming of the next holiday. It will keep you sane in-between. That and gin!

Mad Mammies at Dawn, Go, Go, Go!

I write this still amazed and dazed that on my first day off after a few long nursing shifts I dragged myself out of bed earlier than a workday to go shopping! Yes, I have now earned my badge and am part of the crazy, bargain hunting mad mammies of the Next sales. Egged on by one of my fellow mad mammy best buds that told me, 'I had to do it just once to observe the madness', I decided to give it a go. That and the fact that I had browsed online the night before, my darling princess/superhero had spied a winter coat that she just thought was cool and I had promised I would get her (I know – very silly in hindsight to promise this, especially as I later learned that coats are a main attraction and sometimes go like wildfire). Albeit I drew the line at getting up so early that I had to line outside amongst the 'hard-core bargain hunters'. Yes, this group had probably set two alarms and had a timetable of how to hit this shop with military precision. I passed these mad mammies heading to their cars laden with bags at 6.15am, the satisfaction of a job well done etched on their faces as I was just heading into the unknown...

Now, usually at stupid o'clock in the morning the roads would be quiet and retail store car parks vacant – not on these days though. I began my journey to the store trying to encourage myself to not listen to the little voice inside shouting 'Get back to bed, you mad woman' and so I cranked up the radio to drone it out. The song I'm So Excited by The Pointer Sisters blared out around my loyal Vicky Fiesta (yup, as I said, we name our cars. She suits Vicky being black in colour and sophisticated looking, ha!) and I couldn't help but become a little excited at this new experience, tinged with a bit of anxiety at the fear of the unknown. The feeling you get when you're heading on your holidays but mixed as in with an exam you have actually prepared for but not knowing if that stuff will come up. I am sure those amongst you whom partake in this madness would probably know this feeling well. I entered the car park and it was like a typical midday Saturday scene as the place was buzzing, crammed with cars and many a mad mammy was spied darting to their cars laden by the big sales bags that were the same size as some of them. I actually had a nervous giggle as it looked like I was observing a weird Pac-Man game but with humans. Luckily, I was provided with top-secret information by a fellow mad mammy who persuaded me to attend, on a certain parking area (although I was told to never reveal these details and, from the crazed look she had when this info was shared, I am sworn to secrecy. Sorry).

I approached the store a little bemused that the queues I was expecting at the door where not to be seen, as it was only 6.15am! I immediately thought Eek, perhaps I should have got up earlier and anxiety arose that the coat I promised to my superhero/princess would be gone. I entered the store and, again, had to stifle a giggle at the Pac-Man-type scene presented. Now, usually in a shop if it is in anyway packed it is quite noisy, but what amazed me is that the sound level for the amount of people present was minimal. They all seemed to focus on the task in hand; concentration etched on many a face. I actually felt a complete novice on what I should be doing as everyone in front of me had massive clear bags that already were busting with items (again, that little voice in my head was asking me, 'Why didn't I bring a bag? Why didn't my fellow mad mammy tell me this vital info?' I felt a bit unprepared in front of these professional bargain shoppers). For the first few minutes I wandered aimlessly along the aisles, a little overwhelmed and underprepared for how to tackle this type of shopping. The nerd in me was thinking You have not researched this enough, you fool and my brain was storing this information for future sales shops, i.e. the New Year sales. I was pulled from my daydream by the friendly face of my friend's sister who imparted the information that settled my fears. "We have the coat that Hannah was looking for." Suddenly, wee explosions of delight went off in my brain. It felt like my goal had been accomplished and suddenly I felt calm and I relaxed, not suffocated by all the rails of clothing. We bid farewell to each other with the plan to meet up for breakfast afterwards.

I began to settle into this shop and actually started to enjoy the madness. I then spied my fellow mad mammy friend and my eyes fell to the floor at her over spilling bag of goodies and I actually laughed out loud. Giving her a little tap on the shoulder she spun round and that look was there on her face that was on many and, if am honest, probably mine too. The looks of 'isn't this great 'craic'' and 'look what I got for my precious minions'. She handed over the coat she had kept for me and another bigger size imparting the information. 'Buy both and see which one fits her', my friend suggested, 'you can bring back the other next week'. Wow, who knew? In these quick and frenzied exchanges of 'hello', 'thanks' and further secret tips that, again, I cannot divulge we parted ways to meet again later for breakfast with her sister. I also learned that the big plastic bags were handed out at the door but as I was a latecomer at 6.15am(!) I could just ask a staff member. This problem was solved before having to find a staff member by banging into my hubby's friend's wife who was on her way out having purchased her goal of a pair of jeans, who gladly passed on her bag.

I had an hour to browse and as I had already purchased my goal item I leisurely enjoyed exploring the rails and doing secret people watching (like a wildlife programme but with humans, ha!) of the traits of those around me. What I have found is that there are few types of bargain shoppers. First, there are the 'hardcore bargain hunters' that I saw already leaving with their goods as I arrived. They get up early, queue and are first in. With military fashion they have covered all areas and the requisite items have been selected. It is all done and dusted in record time. The second, whom I found the most amusing, are the 'hunter-gatherers'. This type can work solely but work best in packs of two or three. They seem to grab loads of items in sizes that they need. If there is more than one in the pack, they seem to take the age of each child and then meet up to gather at different sections of the shop. They then rummage through and choose from the piles. The concentration on some faces is hilarious, but when you look at their shop you admire their gains and at times have slight envy for it.

Amongst the mad mammies in the kids' section there were speckles of the man species. I observed that their role mainly was to be used as a clothes horse for their female partners and probably were there as the taxi drivers too. In the adult sections there were a few men in suits. In my mind, I assumed they were heading to work after and attempting to spruce up their work wardrobe with some bargains on the way. Really, in this economy, a wise thing to do with the price of suits these days – I actually applauded their efforts even though I acknowledged to myself that even if my hubby dearest had to wear a suit to work there would be no way I would spy him wandering around the men's section at 'stupid o'clock'. His bed is much more important to him. There were also a few of the younger male generation browsing amongst the 'out-out' gear.

I browsed past the ladies section, admiring the purchases of the ladies that were there to spend their exposable income solely on themselves – the sophisticated career ladies, the carefree young ones who throw flowing maxi dresses and holiday gear in their bag, probably in anticipation of sunny holidays. I made my way to the queue that was like a snake around the entire shop and, on the advice of my fellow mad mammy, went to the queue she advised. Here, as a novice, I observed another process I was not familiar with. Later, I was educated over breakfast that this is the elimination stage (yes, my mad mammy friend is a pro at these sales and, if honest, she would agree becomes a little manic with the anticipation of them). Apparently, when you are happy that you have gathered enough, sorted through them and divided your gatherings if working in groups before you join the checkout line, you have a final elimination stage. I watched as across the store, bags were again emptied on the floor and with concentration once again etched on faces, items were inspected more closely and if passed, they proceeded to the checkout. Those that failed at this stage were put on nearby rails and sometimes, as soon as they were left, another shopper who had spied them from a distance would adopt the item(s).

I stood in the queue having mulled over my items, all of which were for lady Hannah and of course, the obligatory item for Mr Henry (yes, he is lucky to have me and it also keeps him sweet, ha!) and after checking time I smugly felt proud that I was on time to collect Hannah from her daddy at his work car park and, with the help of my mad mammy friend, I had accomplished the goal of the trip to purchase the 'cool winter coat' for our princess/superhero.

The last task was completed with the help of a lovely staff member of helping me get my bag ready for checkout. She expertly laid my bag on the floor, sorted the tags, etc, and divided the items required for scanning – all with friendly banter. We had a giggle when I explained I was a 'novice' at this and she ended it by saying, 'You will be hooked now' – eek! I am sure that the staff must be the only ones that dread these sales – hats off to them. They were very efficient, helpful and professional even though I am sure they had been on the go-to late last evening and up even earlier than the 'hardcore bargain hunters'. Adrenaline is an amazing thing and I am sure by the end of the working day those poor staff will maybe have all the intentions of a celebratory drink for surviving the sales, but I bet a lot will be fast asleep by the second!

Afterwards, we met up for breakfast with Hannah and enjoyed pancakes and coffee in McDonald's while Hannah played on the computers. When did that ever happen? Probably the fact I usually just use drive-thru and am never up at 'stupid o'clock'. I was very impressed by their breakfast, coffees and computers though!

I reflected on the dawn shop as I drove home. I observed Hannah in the rear-view mirror grinning like a Cheshire cat as she insisted on wearing her 'cool new winter coat' even though it is July (although we are in Ireland so she could get the use out of it). When we got home I watched how she excitedly tried on her other clothes, especially the Star Wars gear and the 'big girl jeans with back and front pockets and cool badges' (oh, to be newly five and easily contented). Yes, I thought, it is still madness that I got up at 'stupid o clock' to go shopping on my day off! (especially when the shopping was not even for me).

I have to agree it was an experience and did give me a giggle with the added bonus that, with my mad mammy friend's help, my goal of purchasing the 'cool coat' was successful. I get that the bargains are good and that it might be mad, but smart moves economically, especially for families with lots of kids, the savings would add up. Am I hooked? I wouldn't say hooked but I do think I would go again but would draw the line at the Boxing Day sales. I will leave that to the 'hardcore bargain shoppers' because the only reason I would be up at that time on Boxing Day is if I am unfortunately working and if I am off I intend to spend it snug in bed, happy with what Santa has brought and will have no regrets that I may have missed a bargain – or will I? Eek!

Not Too Posh to Pump, Just Frazzled

The ole debate on the subject about 'women drivers' – once the lid is opened it's like Pandora's box. I bet my hubby is shouting obscenities at the screen as he reads this (such a keeper I have). Now, before I go on further with my tale I do believe that, really, there is no official winner of this title. I believe that there are good male and female drivers and also there are some very bad male and female drivers. Sometimes on the road you do feel like you are doing a hazard perception course, but a bit of courtesy and patience goes along way. This is especially towards learner drivers as we have all been there although some forget and show no sympathy towards this category – shame on you! You know who you are!

I love driving and had a great instructor who was patient, humorous and probably a wee bit pleasantly mad (although I am sure in his profession these traits are invaluable). He found it very amusing that when learning to drive I also read books on the practical skills before my lessons (yup, once a nerd always a nerd). That and the fact that once in a lesson I was banged into at the back by my father-in-law (well, at the time future father-in-law). Now, what are the odds of that happening? Very low, I think, but he again reversed into me in a car park when I was parked(!) a few years later. Yup, you couldn't write it, well, I am now. We actually get on so it wasn't as if he was trying to bump me off. It took him a long time to live this one down. I was also very nervous before my actual test and ended up doing the test wearing my driving instructor's wife's reading glasses. Why? Due to my nervousness the characters on number plates kept jumping about even though my eyesight was fine then. The glasses made them bigger and easier to read so I had to keep them on for entire lesson so as not to look strange (always a drama).

I especially value my licence since becoming a mad mammy; it is invaluable. It has sometimes been the best baby soother ever and many a night in the baby stages I drove for ages until the little minion had fallen asleep. I can state though, that the cleanliness and state of the inside of my car has deteriorated since 'Mammyville'. When inspecting fellow mad mammy's cars I don't feel so bad as theirs often resemble mine... My car pre-Hannah was always spotless, washed and gleaming, had air fresheners changed regularly, had lovely clean seats, floors immaculate and the boot was always empty and clean. Post-Hannah my car has become neglected and abused by my darling minion. It is scattered with her toys, clothing and books. When I do get to clean the backseat I always find carcasses of food, etc. Sometimes when I walk towards her at work I feel bad at how neglected it looks and I feel as if it is looking back at me as if to say 'wash me, please'. It may not be as pristine as pre-Hannah but it is indeed an important accessory to my mad mammy sanity. I am making a mental note to wash and vacuum her tomorrow as I type. Well, perhaps sweet-talk my hubby to do it for me as he is much better; well, that's what I tell him.

The reason I have been thinking on this subject is that on my way home last night my worst fears occurred. I conked out on the main road into town at the traffic lights to Sainsbury's. I know, cringe... Now, the reason for my breakdown wasn't the malfunction of the engine, electrics, etc, but no, even more shameful, the malfunction of me not remembering to top up the diesel! In my defence I had planned to swap cars with the hubby at lunchtime, but again, this mad mammy forgot and drove back to work. I only realised I was in trouble when it began chugging and the nurse I was giving a lift to commented on same – oh, the shame. Have I ever gone into the red zone and drove on for a bit? Yes, I have, as I am sure a lot of honest readers would agree. Even my hubby has although he would never admit. I thought I would get home and sort it tomorrow. Well, to all those that in the past have told me 'Aye, you will be grand, you have so many miles left, blah blah'... It's untrue, so be aware.

Now, to add insult to injury my phone-a-friend aka hubby did not answer my SOS call. Typically, this is the man that usually has his mobile surgically stuck to him and is the one giving off about people with mobiles who never answer, hmm... It's like the saying 'the pot calling the kettle black'. Thankfully, after advice from my passenger (whom I'm sure will not be asking for a 'lift' again) I attempted to start Vicky Fiesta up again. The heavens must have been watching as she gave me a wee lifeline of a few more metres and with a random turn, I managed to park her half in and half out of the garage. My manoeuvre was met with a look from a male driver exiting the garage of both horror and amusement. So, of course, I explained to him my dilemma that in turn made his amusement increase to laughter. Although he did offer to push and I accepted his help with the banter of 'women drivers' blah blah; as I did kind of deserve it for this mistake. I never got his name but I am thankful and glad that the world still has good Samaritans speckled through it. I would also like to say that, thankfully, I still had ten euros lying in my bag, as I did not have my bank card on me. The garage assistant further highlighted my car cluelessness by shouting over the tannoy not once but twice to 'just hold the pump in owner of the black Fiesta' (much to the amusement of my passenger who was relaying the incident to her other half on the mobile. She was to get a takeaway on the way home but due to my scenic route she was now making alternative eating arrangements with her partner).

Finally, after getting further assistance from another member of staff (that at first I thought was marching towards me to tell me off) she explained that if you let your car run out of diesel it fills with air and is hard to pump at first. There ye go, another nugget of information I am gladly sharing from my misdemeanour. So to all who observed the mad mammy making crazy moves with her car and being shouted at over the tannoy, I had just finished a 12hr nursing shift and yes, very silly to run out of diesel. I was not getting my gas pumped as was too 'posh to pump' – more 'too frazzled to pump', ha!

Of course, when I was back on the road again, calamity resolved, it was then that my SOS call was returned by my hubby (some superhero he was...) Yes, he did shout obscenities and then find it totally amusing but, hey, I hold my hands up and say I deserve it. I also defend my actions as in the world of juggling, work, house, kids and putting up with a man, we mad mammies do forget things from time to time. Yes, even important things like feeding the car and that's OK. No one died or suffered injury due to my forgetfulness (in fact, I caused a raise in endorphins in my fellow drivers by their sniggers and laughter as they learned my error, so I really gave their moods a boost on their drive home!) I used my driving knowledge straight away: the wee hazard triangle was pressed to alert others of my stationary position and, thanks to my prayers being answered and a Good Samaritan and helpful garage assistants, the gift of diesel arrived to my thirsty Vicky Fiesta. Will this help keep me alert to the little gas light on the car in future? I certainly hope so. I can't say for definite as, hey, I'm a mad mammy.

I would say that humour did help me not to lose the plot too much or panic and lose my patience, which I am sure would have done the situation no good. I believe that this is one of the other most powerful tools that us mad mammies/career ladies, in fact, all women possess. To any out there who are having a bad day or recovering from a hellish day, laugh in the face of adversity. Yup, great big belly laughs and then straighten your invisible superhero cape that all ladies possess and go to the fridge and pour a glass of wine. Because we all know that humour and wine is a double whammy power.

THINKING OUT LOUD

For the last few days I have been thinking about what our kids really need. The running joke in our house is that we are always moving from our 'starter home' (well, I am, my hubby, as the saying goes, 'easy going tan!' and happy with what he has, is the problem). Now, the house we are in is grand and we have many great memories of moving in that cold December night thirteen years ago and feeling like proper grown-ups. We loved knocking walls down and showering love on this house that needed a lot of TLC and a lot of help from Granda Harry (a joiner by trade and was well used by us). This doesn't mean I can't dream of a big garden that I can let Hannah run riot in and have a wee area for the adults, especially me, a nice little summerhouse tucked in the corner that in my dreams I can write wee books at my leisure on a distressed white desk in a snug little area with soft furnishings and scatter cushions. It will have a driveway that both our cars can fit in; no more communal parking areas (yes, I am a dreamer and dramatic but, hey, my dreams so I'm allowed). Yes, you may say, 'Sure, these dreams are not out of reach and could be achieved'. This is where my hubby, aka voice of doom, negativity and probably reason, if honest, always puts a slant on the move.

He comes up with points such as: 1) What if we move to the dream house and you have neighbours from hell? 2) That Hannah has no friends and as we have such a small mortgage now, why not use our disposable income to continue going on holidays and family days away? The bricks and mortar point, always a sticking point (one that always wins and then we book a holiday).

When I reflect on my childhood we never spent much time in our garden. Once you got to the age that you were allowed to enter the 'square' you thought your life was complete. You got to play in an area in the middle of your street that was the place to be. This was really your back garden. The summers were days of playing rounders that seemed to last all day. The shed walls were the courts of many ball games; the chattering of the ball game rhymes I can still recall: 'One, two three a leary, ten girls' names I used to know...' The sound of balls hitting the kerbs as the 'Padsy' games took place. The sound of laughter as we swung around the lamppost on long lengths of rope and a cushion you sneaked from your living-room to make it more comfortable. The nights spent camping out on the green areas around the street. Telling ghost stories, having midnight feasts and playing Truth or Dare?

The memories of entering 'Teenageville' and how you ventured out of the street; exploring the back roads behind our street; yes, even experimenting with the odd alcoholic beverage and investigating the old abandoned houses that were supposedly haunted and dead man's alley. Daffodil stealing and walks with your first boyfriends all took place in the areas around your street. All innocent and safe fun; we were not bothered whether we had a big garden, a big driveway or summerhouse.

Really, I think that sometimes parents – mad mammies like me – concentrate too much on what we think our kids need and what they really need. When Hannah reached the big age of five she was given the freedom to the back street (really a lane that runs the length of our row of houses). To her, this privilege was worth its weight in gold. She now knows that other kids her age live on this row and also they too have been given the freedom of the back street. The sound of laughter that echoes when they are out there, flying up and down on their flickers, playing 'zombies' and chalk games for hours on end brings it back to me that really, a house is really just bricks and mortar and a home is what you make it whether it be a big house in the country, a semi with a drive or a house on an estate that has a back lane. Our garden in which we attempted to create a play area for Hannah and a wee seating area for the BBQ king, aka the hubby, and us serves its purpose. It is a little suntrap; it is not the big garden of my dreams but with my fake hedging to aid privacy, it is a wee oasis on a warm day. The only time Hannah really uses it is if her friends come in but she mostly enjoys the lane at the back (typical, but I'm sure we would be the same if we had that big garden). Her priority is having friends and exploring, climbing and falling off the walls out the back, climbing the tree at the bottom of the row, making muddies and playing pretend shops.

Life can change in an instant, tragedies occur and families are changed forever. It is when you see this happen that you can't help but re-assess your life. You see what is really important. The materialistic side is forgotten and you appreciate what the real gems in your life are. That for most is family, good friends and a happy home, no matter what the packaging. Yes, it is fine to dream of bettering your life, having joy at getting that new sofa, kitchen, computer, etc – we are only human, although sometimes we can become too wrapped up in the materialistic side of life and a reality check now and then does bring you back to earth with a bump.

When discussing this in recent days a point was brought up that when family or friend disputes occur, should we really forgive people who have hurt us? Life is so short. One response was 'no' but what we should do is, if we have had toxic relationships we should let ourselves know that it is better to let them go and move on. Sometimes some bridges can't be mended and accepting this for all parties is much healthier than enduring more heartache.

Yes, I am feeling somewhat reflective and blessed for what I have this week. There are many things I wish I had been blessed with and that have caused me to feel sorry for myself from major issues to dramatic ones, but as I have said, we are only human and that's OK. The powerhouse of this mad mammy in recent times has attempted to process Why have I not been blessed with another child? A thought that I now accept is fine and what will be will be. We are blessed with Hannah and others are not so lucky. I have also toyed with bad thoughts towards a snoring hubby and the wish for a silent sleeping one, ha! Again, this is fine. We all wish that we had a family or an extended family that got on well all of the time, but life is not like that so we accept this, do our best and enjoy and appreciate what we have. Mainly I am blessed with two fabulous parents that I know are precious commodities and to those who, in this crazy world may not value this point, I urge you to do so and to spend time with them. Share your kids with them. Grandparents are so important and when relationships break down, never use them as weapons.

Yesterday, Hannah used our curtain and attempted to fly like a superhero – the result was a bent pole and a tearful child explaining the need to do this as a part of her 'mission'. Now, of course, my first reaction was not all warm and fuzzy but when I looked at her wee face I couldn't stay mad for long. The pole was fixed by the fixer-upper of all things in Hannah's eyes – her daddy. When our little princess/superhero was tucked up in bed later we laughed at her antics and paused to think that these are the memories that we will re-tell in the future and laugh at like the memories we re-tell of our family antics. I am sure my siblings remember the drama when my little brother Harry let the bath run over while playing on his computer. When the water began dripping from the light in the kitchen, Granda Harry exploded. The electric was turned off and we were all summoned to the kitchen; towels were handed out and the brush was used to release the avalanche of water. Daddy stormed out for a walk to calm down and not to kill Harry and we all helped Mum mop up in the dark shouting at Harry. This story now, years later, makes us giggle.

Life's a journey or more like a rollercoaster – the ups and downs and the happy and sad times are what makes it real. How we react and adapt is up to us. I still believe humour is our best armour in the face of adversity. Life can be unfair; it can make you question 'why?' If there is a God he lets bad things happen, especially to good people although all we can do is keep getting up and fight through the bad, sad and hard times. Lean on our family and friends, enjoy spending time with them and never feel bad when relationships sour

– sometimes we have to accept that this is the way it is and move on.

So, does this mean I will stop having my leisurely 'gleeks' at 'Property Pal' on-line and give up on the hope of moving and that my hubby stops snoring? Hell, no. Will it happen in my lifetime? Umm, not sure but there are some lovely nice bungalows in Greencastle that would be ideal for our retirement when Hannah flies the nest (can't give up on my dreams, life would be boring). Don't sweat the small stuff, people, although it is hard to do in this crazy world. Reality checks from time to time are good but never stop dreaming. Why? Dreaming is good for the soul and in them you can be married to a non-snorer briefly – helps you cope with reality.

TINY FOOTPRINTS FOREVER ETCHED ON OUR HEARTS

I write this with an ache that always thumps that little harder when the anniversary of the death of our son Jacob comes around. As explained in the Dedication, even though it will be ten years this September 26th that we said hello and goodbye at the same time, anniversaries always tend to make you feel raw. You remember every detail of that time, the names of the nurses, the doctors; the kind words, the not so kind words. The moment your world stood still when they said, 'I'm sorry, you're going into labour and your baby will die'. The scream that is released from your body that you don't even realise is your own, it sounds so animalistic and broken. It always seems to run like videotape at that time of year. He was our precious baby boy, Jacob, who was born very premature and didn't survive the birth. Now, I questioned whether I should write on this subject and then decided this is the reason why this subject is still a taboo. People are afraid to discuss their loss for fear of making people feel uncomfortable or look like they are weird for talking about their dead child.

This is where I want to try and explain and educate why this taboo must be broken. When you have carried a child for many months, you pass the three-month mark and your fear of early miscarriage settles. I, too, have suffered miscarriages, it hurts and you have to grieve, but when you get further on and let yourself attempt to enjoy the pregnancy and then you experience stillbirth or, like us, go into early labour and then lose that baby, the grief is beyond words. To labour to silence is horrendous and to bury your baby is beyond comprehension, unless you have had to endure this yourself. Now, I understand that this is a hard subject for people to understand and so they ignore it or avoid their friends and family that this has happened to. I, through research (yes, the nerd in me was there in happy and sad times) discovered that many people lost friends due to this and this I found sad. I believe this was probably more to do with not having the knowledge on this subject to deal with this tragedy and if the taboo was lifted then it could cause less heartache for all.

The first few months are horrendous and your grief is all-consuming as sometimes you don't want to see anyone – I know I didn't. I never left the house for six weeks apart from the funeral and after that I shopped outside of town. You are so raw that it seems you see babies everywhere. Once we abandoned our trolley in a supermarket as everywhere we turned there seemed to be new babies. Through these hard days what gave us comfort were the cards we received from friends and family, the text messages and the friends being on the other end of the phone to be a listening ear. Of course, you also have to deal with the heartache of your friends and family being pregnant and going on to have their healthy babies. This is hard, but what we need to educate is that, yes it hurts, but a couple who have lost their baby is grieving for their own, they don't want to have anyone else's, so even though their hearts are breaking they are happy for their friends and family – they are just bereft that they cannot have their own baby.

When we lost Jacob one of my best friends was also pregnant and due at the same time. I worried so much that our friendship would not survive this and that I would not be able to deal with it. At the time she was in another country but came home before the birth. The day she was home I drove past her house and then instinctively went round the roundabout and knocked at her door (she had told me 'no pressure to visit', that she understood). Why did I visit? Because I knew our friendship was worth it; I knew that she was heartbroken for us but that she was having a baby and this was a great thing. We hugged and I held it together and yes, I cried when I got home but for the future that would not be of bringing up our babies together, etc. I held her baby when he arrived and the comfort you get you cannot measure, although again, I held it together and when I got home I cried with my husband. I cried again for what should have been. This is normal though and helps you heal. We are still great friends and before she left to go back home we drank wine, cried for the memories of being mad mammies together that would never be, but it was a lovely night. We laughed and got through it. I understood more how she was feeling and she got me. Yes, when I see her gorgeous boy growing into the right wee lovable terror that he is I do sometimes get the ache that 'Aw, why couldn't I have my own wee terror here too?' but this is a normal feeling and I get it. Life is unfair at times but letting your feelings out helps.

Since we lost our precious boy I have known a good friend who also lost her baby boy to stillbirth and another who, again, due to a premature birth lost her boy. Recently, I have seen two mothers lose their precious babies to heart defects and medical reasons in our own wee town. Every time I hear of a child predeceasing their parents my heart aches; I remember that awful dark place that you are plunged into and I pray for those families to get through this awful time. I admire greatly when I see how families that have gone through this loss rally together and put their grief to good use, campaigning for different charities in memory of their loved ones and raising awareness. You see, what people don't realise is that when you lose a baby/child it is not only the parents that are bereft, but also a ripple effect goes across the whole family and close friends. Families are your support network and feel the pain you are going through. They also feel helpless, especially your parents. They see your hurting and can't fix it although what they need to know is that just being there is all they need to do. If they want to cry, cry with them; if they're angry and want to hit things, give them a pillow or an annoying family member (joking! Well, if a family member is willing, let them, ha!) This brings me to your greatest armour in the face of adversity – humour.

As previously mentioned because I feel so strongly about it, I believe humour in our darkest days got us through. You have to hang onto the humour. I still have a vivid memory of my hubby always trying to get me to eat in the weeks after losing Jacob. I was just so sad that I had no need for food. Anyway, one day he made a curry and I attempted to eat a bit. He came in and was pushing the curry around and hardly eating, left the fork down. I suddenly snapped and shouted at him for not eating and him badgering me to eat, blah blah. When I had finished my tearful rant he looked at me and said,

'It's too hot, am letting it cool'. We both just looked at each other and burst out laughing. You have to let laughter back in. It is the glue that will mend you. Yes, you will still have days when your heart bursts with sadness but it gets easier. One of my best friends made me laugh on the saddest day of my life when, after the funeral, she apologised for her choice of flowers. I looked down and she had the most gorgeous bunch of sunflowers. She proceeded to chatter on, saying she just didn't know what to buy and thought she had now made the wrong choice. When she finally looked up at me we just burst out laughing – hers in a nervous way, probably thinking I was going to lunge at her. For me, it lightened the moment in an awful time and now, whenever I see sunflowers it makes me smile. They were a perfect choice.

You see, when you lose a child in pregnancy or in early years you are not only grieving their loss but of the milestones you will miss – their first day at school, their first tooth falling out, their first communion, confirmation, passing their driving test and going to university/first job. The list is endless. I remember someone who, meaning well, said that it was perhaps better to lose him at birth than a few years down the line, as it would be harder. I actually laughed out loud at this and explained to her that I will grieve every milestone whether he had lived two years or one month. She didn't think on it like that until I had explained but then, as I said, if you have never been in that position, why would you?

We set balloons off every year with our rainbow baby Hannah and Dylon. We do this to acknowledge that he was here and that Hannah grows up with a healthy idea of death, etc. As explained earlier, she understands that he lives in heaven with his Granny Margaret and recently drew a picture of heaven with his name and two figures of me and her looking up, waving. Her daddy was not in the picture so obviously that means I'm her favourite. We have the picture framed in her room and she is very proud especially as she was able to spell his name.

Really, what I want to say from sharing this is that educating the public is the way to go and that to break the taboo is a great healer for families going through this loss. We love to be able to speak of our babies and so you should never be uncomfortable. Remembering helps heal the tiny footprints forever etched on our hearts. There is not a day goes by that I don't think of my baby – he is always my first and last thought. This does not mean that I talk about him every day but if I do or you meet someone who has lost a child, never shy away from the topic if they bring it up. This means they want to talk and feel comfortable to share it with you.

When people used to say to me, 'You have an angel now,' that used to drive me mad. I know that it was meant well but I used to go home and shout to myself saying, 'You have a blooming angel? I just want my baby!' Now I'm further down the line I get it and I do believe we will meet again. It brings me comfort and, from someone who is not holy, I have more time for faith now but on my terms.

I also learned that we have moved on from years ago where you were not given time with your baby and they were buried in unmarked graves – so sad. I have three aunts that lost their babies in late pregnancy and, to this day, they still feel emotion regarding it. When I was going through this, one aunt couldn't face me to begin with as she said it brought it all back. I needed to talk to her and when I did we cried. She too could relive every aspect of that time, the doctors, nurses, etc.

The heartbreak she felt of not being able to see or hold her baby and it being whisked away still stays with her. She does not know where he is buried and this has also never left her. This shows you it never leaves you. Really, you just live a different kind of normal. There are still areas for lots of improvements that could be done in maternity services to support this loss and I definitely feel that having mental health nurses on these wards would be of huge benefit.

I also believe that to go through this and survive takes a normal kind of person that, due to no fault of their own, is forced to become a superhero and has to learn to fight to get back on track, be that as a team or on their own. Sometimes relationships break down and I get that also. We grieve at different times and methods and sometimes it is just too hard. We used to say we would fake it till we make it. Whatever way you get through this is up to you. I just hope that the world starts to realise that it is OK to talk and that this has the healing power to help. I take my hat off to Sands and other support networks for grieving parents. They provide literature and face to face groups that definitely helped us. Grief is like a journey and at times you are battered by storms and knocked over by tidal waves but you can survive. You just have to fight and it used to drive me mad when my mum used to say this, but she was right. Even though you no more want to fight, you hurt so bad you have to. Why? Because you deserve to be happy, we only have one life and I'm sure your baby would not want you to waste it while you're here.

My advice to anyone reading this or who knows someone going through this is to talk, listen and write your feelings down in the early days. My mood diary got me through and showed me how I was getting better. I still have it along with all Jacob's blankets, photos and footprints, etc. It shows me how we have survived. Although the cape of humour is also a vital tool and you must wear it diligently in the early days it will get you through your darkest days. It'll sometimes be mixed with tears in the early stages, but that's OK. Tears help heal and always remember to do something every year to acknowledge your baby. When we let balloons go we watch Hannah running along, urging God to let them into heaven for Jacob – it makes us smile with a tinge of sadness. He lives on in this legacy and will be forever entwined in the tapestry of our life. We are different people because of him but hopefully better people who have empathy. We get that sometimes people's actions may hide a lot of pain behind closed doors. Life is a rollercoaster so hold on tight and we hope that our future has little dips and no upside down ones.

Storms Bring Rainbows

Well, today as I was doing the normal household chores I banged into my laptop bag hanging on the kitchen chair. It was with that knock that I realised that through all the damn minefields in this crazy world that have knocked me, I have got through them by writing it all down. I know through my own nurse training how beneficial it is letting out what is in your head; it frees your mind, it's cathartic, it helps you process and gain closure to move on. When you let things fester or ignore issues then they become toxic which is not good for the mind, body or soul.

You see, I think the reason I have avoided writing about this particular mad mammy moment is that I know when I let it out I have acknowledged that it was real, that it happened and that it hurts, although I have also got to the point where I know it means that I am healing and that is surely a good thing.

If I rewind to October 2016, the Henrys were in a good place, a fabulous place in fact. Lawrence had a new job in an area that he loved albeit involved more travel but we could work around that – life was good. The step-teenager of the house was still in his 'plonker' stage but we were all having a united parents/step-parents front in trying to tackle this chapter, so it all felt under control. It got even better when I found out I was pregnant – woo-hoo! It had been a good few years of wishing for this moment and one we embraced excitedly but nervously due to my history. We stayed positive and had great support from our GP. We kept the news close to us, only telling our parents and few family members. Due to the nature of my work they also had to be told and we were so touched at how people responded. They knew how much this meant to us and we knew they all had us in their prayers.

Rewind to the end of October 2016 and, in the space of a few weeks, this all changed and is where the happiness ended. We found out that I had an ectopic pregnancy and was admitted for surgery. I have been very open of my history of miscarriages and losing our precious boy Jacob, but when you experience an ectopic it knocks you so differently. My first thought was sadness, seeing a heartbeat on the screen and being told it is in the wrong place and cannot continue. Secondly, you feel anger as to why God would let this happen in letting me get pregnant when I was just coming to the point of accepting it may not happen again. Giving us hope and then taking it back. It seemed so cruel and unfair as we had so much to give and it seemed that people who either didn't want kids or didn't deserve them could fall pregnant so easily. Lastly, you have to get your head around the fact that you have to end this pregnancy surgically or it could be fatal to you. Effectively, you had to terminate your baby before it could harm you. Hard to process for sure; your head knows it's right but your heart aches.

I had heard of ectopic before but had never had the fear of experiencing; more so, miscarriage played on my mind with my history. What I did know I didn't seem to display in terms of any of those symptoms you associate such as pain in shoulder, extreme pain, heavy bleeding, etc. I felt pregnant and a bit achy but nothing that worried me. Little did I know that sometimes that can be the nature of this, that some experience a lot of obvious symptoms whereas others, like me, don't and then it comes on at lightning speed. The latter happened to me as, that morning when waiting to go to surgery, I became faint on my way back from the bathroom. Luckily my hubby heard my calls and got to me before I collapsed. I was experiencing a ruptured ectopic pregnancy and yes, I felt pain then. This followed a very scary few hours of emergency surgery – laparoscopic surgery abandoned for full abdominal surgery – removal of a tube and two blood transfusions. I woke up feeling battered and bruised and really quite numb. I heard a lot of 'you were very lucky', etc. Again, the irony of the sentiments at that time didn't sink in. Yes, there were a few things that, in hindsight, we felt needed to be addressed and that have been highlighted, but at that moment we were just numb.

So, yeah, the last few months went from a mood of elation to deflation for us as a couple. Poor Law has been left traumatised and I have had to deal with the aftermath of abdominal surgery recovery without the joy of a baby to help distract from the pain – hard on the heart for sure. My big 40th birthday came and went with civil celebrations, as I was too poorly to enjoy. That will be rectified and I have a twin brother, hubby and lots of family and friends waiting in the wings to celebrate with me soon. Yes, we have been through another crappy minefield but when I reflect from the position

I am at now I can see the positives. I am physically on the mend and now just healing my 'wee heart' that takes a bit more time. I am glad I reached my vintage age and am here to tell the tale. It would have been a shame to leave the world in my 30s and ruin my poor twin's day. I have a lot of living left to do and age is really just a number that should be celebrated as there are a lot of people who don't reach many milestones. We have Hurricane Hannah that we are thankful for everyday, others are still waiting for their miracle babies (well, most days. if you're keeping it real as sometimes, kids – even the most wanted – can cause mad mammy meltdowns). I have a stepson whom I know will turn out right once he gets over these 'plonker' years and will turn into the lovely boy again we all helped raise. Humour has once again been ignited and has helped bolster us through this storm.

My twin relayed that he was grateful I survived as it would have spoiled his birthday buzz and he presented me with a nice, hot water bottle to help with recovery. Now, what you need to know is that my twin is quite the Scrooge with money, so when he bought a nice, fancy, hot water bottle, not a pound shop one, you know he cares. He also explained that it was cheaper than a wreath, so bargain! Yup, that's why I'm the nurse and he is not. It was what I needed – laughter! It does indeed lift you in your darkest times.

I also saw how, no matter what age you are, that to your mammy, you will still be her baby. If you hurt, she hurts too. I guess I got that when I saw wee Granny Ann sit at my bedside in hospital and become emotional. She was sad for us but also glad I was here and I got that in that moment. We lightened the mood as I told her I couldn't get up at present to hug her and if she kept crying, I would, but that it hurts my tummy if

I do, so she came to me. We hugged and that was how it went. In the weeks that followed, as Law had only just started his new job, Hannah and I had a sleep-over at Mum's to be near her school. My sister, Laura, shared her king-size bed with Hannah for few days (before wanting to kill her) so I could recover in the spare bed. You see, Hannah is like a koala bear and a noisy, frequent toilet tripping, lip-smacking (gets that from her daddy) nocturnal nightmare and, even in a huge bed, through the night she sought Laura out and latched onto her, sometimes settling on her head, arm, etc. Now, to every mammy and daddy reading this, we get this – we have probably all been there and adapted. To a twenty-something lady used to her comforts with no children, these antics don't make her warm and fuzzy. She doesn't see the five-year-old that rubs her nose so much that it may fall off as 'cute', her snoring as adorable and finally, an alarm at 6.30am as helpful as when she has work in the morning. Did I secretly laugh from the other room when I heard her try and disengage from Hannah's hold in the night and muttered not so sweet nothings when doing so? Yes, I did, but I was also very grateful for her putting up with her for as long as she did and grateful to Auntie Jean who lent us the camp bed when she threw her out and got back into Mammy's room.

I also learned that I love my job and that nurses rock. The care I received in hospital was great. I saw nurses do what I do so often too – they would pop in on their way home to say 'Night' to me and certain other patients to offer reassurance when you are at your lowest and most vulnerable. I have seen what it's like from the other side as a patient and it is eye opening. I was humbled when a nurse from recovery and on the wards called to see how I was the next day. It made me feel glad that in a time when nursing has had bad press and the whole health service is at its knees, there are still people in the job that care. We do think on our patients and not only as a number. Yes, of course, we have to keep our work life separate to cope but it's also refreshing to see that there is nursing with heart still continuing.

It highlighted how precious your family and friends are and when bad things happen you know you can count on them. I have a great group of close friends and we may not see each other as often as we like due to the constraints of this crazy world but, you know, when the chips are down they are there. The texts, calls and chats had not gone unnoticed. I laughed and smiled when I received gorgeous flowers from my work a day after leaving hospital. I laughed because, if you knew my work and how hard it is to organise anything, even a tea kitty, that for them to actually get flowers sent before my return to work is another miracle and did make me chuckle.

So, my mantra from that day was to 'fake it till we make it'. I vowed to embrace the crazy world again. Getting back in the driving seat helped (I'd forgotten how much music in the car is therapy and good for the soul). I allowed my heart to heal at its own pace; when bad days came I wallowed but then got back up again. Hannah was and still is a tonic for this and seeing things through her eyes, you can't help but smile and appreciate life and all that is good. Who knows what the future holds? But, for now I am grateful to be here with my family to enjoy and embrace all that is good in this crazy world.

I shared this to show, warts and all, how life is indeed a rollercoaster and that our fairy tale we all wish for sometimes doesn't pan out in reality. Yes, it is unfair at times but you do get that there are others out there dealing with a lot worse. Life throws minefields at us all but it is in these times that we also see the beauty in this world. That of friendship, family and your partners support all the buoys that we need to stay afloat in stormy weathers. Remember, after the storm – as corny as it sounds – there has to be a rainbow. It's coming, we just have to fight till it's there.

The only way is up and I do encourage those who read this and are going through hard times to use writing as a tool. It may not be in a blog but a piece of paper – empty that head and you will feel better. I have finished this piece in a better place than I started, so give it a go. Writing really is free therapy, well, for me anyway.

To those trying to conceive, never give up. For those that have tried different interventions and it has not worked, I can only imagine your despair and I urge you to think outside the box. There are other ways to become a mammy that can be explored. Sometimes our bodies let us down and it is so hard, frustrating and so unfair. The route may have to change from the conventional, but with hope and fight you can get there.

Date Nights and All That Jazz

Life is busy, we all juggle so many things at times; the day doesn't seem long enough just to do the essentials. Date nights really do go down the list, whether you're a mad mammy, working lady, loving wife or all three! (I hope you're not laughing, beloved one).

I am guilty of spending more of my days off now in my PJs on the sofa at night with the other half and ordering a takeaway and a wee vino/gin and I am as happy as can be. Nothing wrong with that, I think. They say it's contentment, settlement and happiness with your wee family and nest (even though I still have my guilty pleasures of scrolling through 'PropertyPal' for other nests. I am happy in my home and know that as Hannah now has wee friends here, I would be moving on my own at present).

Now that the other half is working further from home it got me thinking that at times we really can be ships passing in the night, especially when the other half is, at present, on nights. You kind of get caught up in the rat race. Doing the school run, kids' after school activities, their friends' birthday parties (that because of their after school activities have grown larger and it seems to be a weekly occurrence). Is it me, or do kids nowadays seem to have better social lives than their parents? Now, I don't see this as a bad thing and yes, activities like swimming lessons are great skills for the kids to learn but you do sometimes end up, due to peer pressure even at a young age, let them join other groups as their 'such and such' friend goes and so the timetable grows. I am happy that they still have interests in outdoor activities as technology has enveloped our kids' minds so early these days, but it's hard to get a balance. Activities such as Gaelic and football clubs help address this balance. My own princess/superhero has just joined the second season of her football club at school. Bonus for both of us as she is in an extra hour on that day so I have an extra hour of 'me' time if I'm off work (although, really, it means doing some kind of household chore, but on the rare occasion I can collide with another mad mammy/friend, etc, it's for a sneaky quick coffee). The hubby goes for a run, as that's his thing.

Although we do put our hands up and admit that we have used tablets as a device to be able to enjoy our dinner when dining out with Hannah, I am sure many reading this have done this as well. We have observed others doing it so we can't be the only ones! Considering the fact that since we have become parents eating out with our child have been our date nights, technology has been embraced so that we all get fed and Hannah has stayed occupied. Fact and double win! You use the tools you have for the greater good of the family and we're sticking to it.

The light bulb moment came recently when our ships passed, the port being my parents' home waiting to collect

Hannah as her school is opposite their house. Law being on nights had not got my message saying I would get our little darling so we had both turned up. In his sarcastic manner, thinking he was funny, made a jokey comment that he would get her seeing as he was the better parent, blah blah. Now usually, I ignore him and my selective hearing is on when he thinks he is funny and I let him live in that dream and curse him in my head. Although on this day I was not on point and my internal thoughts of I hate you when he goes on like the comedian, he wishes he had escaped. Yup, I said it out loud in a room with my sister, mum and beloved – eek. My sister burst out laughing and so did he. I, out of nervousness and disbelief, felt that my internal voice had thrown me under the bus. I don't really hate him like I want to hurt him or lock him in a cupboard and give him no food kind of way – really, I don't. He just grates me like all men do when they go on about balancing kids, chores, work, etc, is 'wee buns' and women make a big deal, blah blah. I am sure ye all have had episodes like this but perhaps won't admit it.

I decided then that perhaps we should try and re-connect, go out for a wee night on our own. In reality, we had to get ourselves out of the couch potato night and go out into the real world – the places where you are not allowed to wear PJs and scraped back hair. We had to introduce date nights into our lives again after nearly eight years of marriage and crazy minefields along the way. I thought perhaps I would remember why I like him more than when I don't. Of course, I love him but, yep, he drives me mad sometimes and I think the basis of this is that we really are in competition with who is the best at juggling the all-star parent, worker and house manager role (love this saying; stole it from my friend who, on a career break raising her kids, gave herself this title when debating with her other half). Due to all that this entails we don't make time for ourselves to have time out together. I am sure this argument would resonate with households all over, even if kids aren't involved. Ladies, we are easily riled when our other half jokes about multitasking and how easy it is; even though we know that we are better we still let them get under our skin. Yes, couch potato land is divine and comfortable, but this too could be seen as getting into a rut and this is not a good thing for mad mammies and our relationships.

Date night was set last week for the next Sunday – last night was the night. My sister is doing placement at Hannah's school so she had agreed to keep her over and take her to school. Saturday arrives and when on my break at work I receive a text saying her school would be closed on Monday as the heating has broken. Seriously! What are the odds? Now, this is where mad mammies have to be strong as, even though I knew a date night was a good thing, that wee voice in my head that loves the couch potato was screaming, 'Cancel! You won't enjoy it when you have Hannah all morning with a delicate head'. I relayed the news to hubby when he was home and I swear I saw a look in his eyes that thought he too was screaming, 'Cancel!' in his head. We both looked at each other and said nothing. We didn't want to be the one to suggest we should cancel. Sunday arrived and a cold Sunday it was, a day that just shouts 'movie and vino/gin!' on the sofa now that Hannah was off school the next day. Evening arrives and I again broached the subject. The hubby was strong; he said he still wanted to go even if it was to be an early night. Damn him I thought, he is good and so I became competitive and thought I will not cancel even though I could feel our comfy sofa trying to reel me in.

The plans changed – my sister would watch Hannah at ours as, even though she loves us, she was not willing to arise at 'stupid o'clock' and entertain Hannah whenever she too had an unexpected duvet day due to the school closure.

I dragged my couch potato-craving body to the bathroom, threw myself begrudgingly into the bath, silently cursing that the hubby hadn't been weak and pulled out. His competitive trait is so annoying.

Two dress changes later and one that the hubby didn't recognise when he arrived back with my sister, until I said. My amused sister highlighted this faux pas immediately, who told him that this was the wrong answer. Yes, they were both black but one was short sleeved with hearts on and the other long-sleeved with stars. He was also wearing his glasses – that's all I'm saying.

Two minutes to nine and we are entering the pub. I have to admit the feeling was nice as we stood at the bar and looked at the cocktail menu. It did feel good to be out as a couple. We were proper adults – not just Hannah's mammy and daddy but us.

I got us a seat, which I was glad about. I admit that as you get older this is more of a necessity and I am not afraid to voice it. The hubby arrived with a berry gin cocktail that was huge and had what looked like a mini Christmas tree as decoration. There was a band playing, the couple opposite were nice and chatty but not stalkers. Life was good. One cocktail down and I heard my name being called but I didn't glance up at first as sure, I'm hardly ever out so obviously not for me. Then I catch a glimpse of a friend from work and gestures of hello are exchanged. I begin to remember that being out as adults is fun and the second cocktail goes down nicely. I begin to look at my hubby as he chats to the random people throughout the night and see the nice guy that he is. Even when he takes to the dance floor and drags me out when Erasure comes on and proceeds to dance like it's 1999 whilst resembling someone suffering a fit, I see the nice, funny guy he is. We ended the night by getting a pizza on the way home and managing first time to flag a taxi outside, result! It was very cold weather and my tired, tipsy body was ready to be reunited with my cosy sofa.

Do I think date nights and all that jazz a good thing? For definite! Research (yes, the nerd in me is out again) backs it up. From what I have glanced at they all strongly reiterate the importance of getting the fun back and spending time together out of the home and away from the stressors of everyday life, what with kids, work deadlines, fertility and health issues, etc. It seems more prevalent as work for most couples and careers is just as important to both. When you add in the mix of kids and all the fun that does to your routine date nights, of course it gets lost in translation. Now, some articles state once a week date nights. I think that's a bit unrealistic in our crazy schedule and work pattern, but I do think at least once a month/every six weeks is best as I still like my couch potato dates, but I do get that seeing your partner out of the home and sprucing each other up should occur more. Yes, we all have flaws and my hubby was always annoying, competitive and a teaser. He always thinks he is right from the time I met him. Our night out reminded me of his fun side, our fun side, aside from being parents (amazing ones, I might add) and coasting through life and all its minefields. We have been through a lot in our marriage but we are still standing, well, we were leaning last night, slightly inebriated.

Now, if you're reading this and bits jump out that make you think When did we last have a date night? Get it on, people. It doesn't have to be the pub, it could be going for a run together, although I will pass on that as the pace my hubby runs, aka Forrest Gump, I would effectively be running on my own anyway, ha! It's really just making a wee bit of time in our busy lives to relax, breathe and realise that the good things of our partners outweigh all the flaws we all have (and if they don't, then – eek!) It could also prevent you having a slip-up and voicing your internal thoughts out loud – kind of awkward...

SHOP BOUGHT AND PROUD

Now, before I begin my wee rant I want to say I love that schools are embracing books and passing onto our kids the joy of reading and capturing their little imaginations. I love this. I remember the absolute joy I gleaned from pouring over my Enid Blyton books, the Malory Towers adventures. When visiting America I indulged in reading my host family daughter's The Baby-Sitters Club series of books. I still have lovely memories of sitting on their swing on the porch on lovely balmy days. When we were constructing our decking in my starter home this was the story behind it. I wanted to get that feeling of sitting in the sun reading a book on my porch. Yes, it is true, the sunny days are few and far between on this Emerald Isle but it has happened and I have enjoyed reading them up until Lady Hannah's arrival.

I remember reading the hardback copy of My Left Foot and Helen Keller in my bed as a ten-year-old, a present from my daddy. I was enthralled and it took me no time to read with the help of a torch under the covers so I could read for longer (yes, I have said I am a nerd and proud even as a child). The book reading has indeed lessened since then as mad mammies don't have as much time as they used to. This is not to say I haven't indulged in a wee quick read when the little darling is at school and I am off work although now my reading is more on the genre of other mad mammies that make me feel normal and give me a giggle when I read of their mad mammy moments in 'Mammyville', or of chick flick books about crazy ladies that also make me feel normal.

I love that Hannah seems to have inherited my love of reading (not hard when her daddy admits his love of reading expands to the two books by Jeremy Clarkson from Top Gear – enough said on that topic). Her stepbrother, Dylon, is not a fan of reading either, much more addicted to the computer world and PlayStation. I should give more credit to Granny Ann for this as she has always read with all her grandchildren and her house always has books that they love to read and read again. She is also the one responsible for taking her to the library for the first time and getting her a library card that she was so proud of (I know – bad mammy – but libraries were not a priority in mad 'Mammyville' for me). Perhaps it's because grandparents are more chilled and have the time to enjoy doing wee trips like this. Either way Hannah wins, so I don't beat myself up about it. It is sad to say that libraries are not being visited as often; probably more to do with the availability of books on-line and cheaper books available to buy now. This is all more enticing and convenient for busy parents than the trek to the library and then the probable fine when you don't remember to return them on time. I wonder if they still do fines. That gives me a flashback of the fines I paid at university – astronomical – especially when you had books over the holidays – eek.

Anyway, I digress and so back to what I wanted to discuss – the fiasco that is World Book Day in my home. My alarm awakened me from my slumber this morning at 8am. Now, I say slumber when really it was more of endurance, as from 4am the silent Ninja sleepwalker had crept into our bed, so I had been crammed between two snorers and Sweaty Bettys, eugh! The beloved hubby would describe it as 'hot stuff'; I disagree. My hubby left for work at 6.30am and I rolled over to his side to get a few hours' sleep and stretch my distorted body. That lasted a nanosecond as when I rolled; the princess/superhero rolled and again, was stuck to my back. What could I do? I did what I am a professional at doing now and balanced on the edge of my bed holding on for dear life and snoozed as best I could. Yes, I admit I silently said bad words about my silent Ninja sleepwalker but that's OK. They were in my head, fleeting, and she will never know.

I grabbed my phone to silence the alarm and with one eye open I saw that I had received a message from one of my fellow mad mammy wingmen. On opening this message I had bad words that I said about her but, again, they were fleeting. No plans made to do her harm, but she did find out as I told her in a text by telling her to go away. Why did I do this? The picture she sent was of a delightful, handmade dinosaur costume for World Book Day. Lovingly painted and accessorised at probably 'stupid o'clock' by my crazy friend. Now, I rang her on my way back from school to slag her off to her face – that's how I am – and was amazed that she said it was easy and, sure, she had bought coloured paper recently, so with the help of Pinterest was 'wee buns' (like, you do not! Well, not in my house anyway!)

Did I look at the picture and think Why can't I be that creative? Yes! I have to admit it again although it was only for a fleeting second. Why? Because I know my limitations and costume making is not one of them. I had a visual of attempting to do so and it was not pretty – the ending was Hannah running away as she was so ashamed of me. I do say, hats off to all ye mad mammies that took out your coloured paper and knocked up amazing outfits, but I also say that you all sicken me and, yes, it is borne out of jealousy for your creativeness and energy to do so. I admit I'm useless creatively and too lazy to try and get better. The duck I attempted to make in woodwork is still somewhere about, mammies, but was supposed to be a child's pulley toy. I think it probably would have frightened a child and I think the Ugly Duckling would have looked liked a beauty queen compared to my attempt. Less said about my attempt to crochet a vest for the poor children of Africa; that didn't work out either and a donation, I'm sure, was much better received than had the vest been sent.

Hannah wished to be Captain America today. As I said, she loves stories about him and so that was easy for me, costume duly bought and, even when we had a slight panic as I couldn't find her book, that was resolved by my fellow mad mammy who let me borrow her son's book (I have to admit that this was the same mammy who did the homemade costume as well. God, she could be annoying if I didn't really like her and need her at times).

This morning, in reality, should have been easy: only one child to dress, no 'faffing' with homemade costumes and probable bits falling off, etc, right? Nope. It had numerous minefields. The costume was put on in slow motion that only five-year-olds can master. Attempts at helping were rebuked as she is a 'big girl' so I internalised my rant and did some high-pitched encouragement talk. I am sure we are all aware of that voice bordering on wanting to explode but holding on as hard as your voice will let you. Finally, her costume was on, hair brushed, which was another minefield and another discussion of how it needed to be in a plait that she can hide as, did I not know Captain America can't have a ponytail? Give me strength.

We only had the shoes and socks to go and we would be out the door. What could go wrong here? Everything! I hear her muttering so I go to investigate in my encouraging mammy voice. I am met by my superhero/princess who is appalled that I have left out Frozen socks for her. "Mammy, Captain America cannot wear Frozen or princess socks." She looks at me in despair as she searches through her drawer for appropriate ones. I try to reason with her, tell her she picked those socks and that they won't be seen under the costume. I only got a look of disgust and then a, "Mammy, I am Captain America today. My princess socks are for another day." Now, at this moment I do have to take a moment and turn away so as not to let her see me silently laughing. Who knew the trials and tribulations of a superhero/princess and her sock choice? Blue socks are found along with her mask that she lost while looking for socks and, after another discussion of how her shoes should be red and not blue like in the book (give me more strength) we are heading for the door.

I am back to happy mammy; my Captain America is dressed with book in hand and will get to school just in time if we leave now. Then the dreaded sentence is said. The one you do not want to hear when heading out the door and your darling is in full costume. Yup, she said she had to pee! Yes indeed, this is when mad mammy exploded. Ranted about why she couldn't use her superhero powers and hold it in till she got to school, as I wrestled to help her get free of costume. I, again, got the look of disbelief and the response of, "Don't be silly, Mammy, it's only pretend!" What can you do but laugh at these moments, eh? Finally, we head out the door after taking the obligatory picture that I had to take twice as she wanted to do the Captain America pose on her knees – whatever! Sorry, this was after a frantic phone call to hubby to see if he knew where my door key was. He obviously was far too busy in an assessment to care and did his professional annoying voice to tell me so. I in turn said "Thank you" in my sweet and annoying voice that really meant 'I hate you'. Admit it, we have all done this.

Anyway, the key appears and I dispatch the superhero to school. When we get there she takes a sudden fit of shyness and has to be coaxed out of the car. I then watch as she decides to take off her mask, the same mask we spent ten minutes looking for earlier. "Give me strength" is muttered again. I watch as she shyly enters the school alongside Elsa from Frozen and Spider-Man (shop bought outfit as well, I may add. In my mind I high-five that mum – she made me feel normal).

I wearily head back to the car and throw myself in, exhausted, and it's only after 9am. I turn to put my seat belt on and catch a glimpse of a fellow mad mammy running with her child who, for today, is Little Red Riding Hood and from the looks of it, not shop bought. It looks fabulous and even funnier as she swings her wee Frozen school bag on her back. Her hoop catches and Little Red Riding Hood is flashing her bloomers unbeknownst to her or her mad mammy. I admit I laugh out loud at the sight and also feel normal that the mammy looks as exhausted as me, but also proud of her attempt and so she should be.

So, happy World Book Day to you all, to those mad mammies that bought shop or created masterpieces. We should all be proud as we survived the madness and can look forward to doing it all again next year. Maybe I will attempt my own creation next year or maybe not, ha! Oh, and perhaps my fellow mad mammy friend that not only lent me her son's book, who also handmade his costume and ultimately won first prize that she joyfully texted me jesting me about, might help me. Although I fear that she has changed so much from this victory that she will want to go bigger and better next year and keep it all top-secret to avoid competition (you know that I am right!) 'Mammyville' is great 'craic', eh? My humour cape is well fastened and ready for the bumps and I advise you all to do the same.

Parents Are a Precious Commodity

In the last few weeks I have pondered on the question of mortality and the meaning of life. Now, I don't want to be morbid or full of doom and gloom but I think that as you get older and see that in turn your parents are also getting older, you do see life in a different light. Then when you become a parent, auntie or uncle you also become transfixed on these little people and the world they have been born into. Now, don't get me wrong, on the whole it is a good perspective that is gained. You see the beauty of the simple things through the eyes of your growing child; you see how this little squishy baby brings joy in a ripple effect throughout your family. I always say if you could bottle the smell of new babies then you would indeed be a rich person. I have loved seeing how Hannah has changed over the years from all the baby stages to toddler and now as a proper superhero/princess at six-and-a-half years old (the half part very important as she likes to point out too often). It is lovely to see her relationship with her grandparents grow although at times it is tinged with sadness that Law's mum is not here to see this. Although as I have said before that we talk of her often, Law re-tells stories from his childhood. Her soup pot is often used and Mum has her duvet cover in her spare room which she calls Granny Margaret's room when Hannah has sleep-overs. Her Granda Lawrence buys her the best ginger nuts; even though I have the same brand, his taste better.

She has just recently got her certificate for stage three in swimming and to her this was like winning the lottery. She now believes she is an Olympic and can't wait to show her skills when we go on holiday end of June. At her training session they divided them into number 1 and 2 groups to learn the different skills. Hannah was not happy at being number 2 and, when asked to wait as she was number 2, she replied, "My daddy said I am always number 1." (Yup, I fear the competitive Henry gene is there. The instructor found this very amusing although Mr Henry tried to blend into the wallpaper). This got me thinking of how, as a child, your daddy is your first superhero. You believe he is the strongest, smartest and the man that knows all the solutions to your problems. You believe every word he tells you, as he knows everything! Even when he tells you that his booster scar is when he fought in Vietnam! So, as gullible school kids you go and re-tell this story to your primary teacher who finds it highly amusing. He was the spider catcher, bike fixer, DIY expert and money man, especially after returning from the pub where you could use your charms to get a few quid for that top you so needed (yes, we have all done this trick, I'm sure). Your mammy is your wing woman for sure and if you needed to butter up your dad to go to the disco or have sleep-overs as you got older it was she who had your back.

Indeed, as we hit our teenage years the parents became the enemy for a bit and the superhero dad was not so popular. He was the stricter parent, especially with his daughters. I still remember the day after slamming my bedroom door as a stroppy sixteen-year-old he took my door off the hinges and can still visualise him walking down the stairs, door on shoulder. I never slammed the door after that and I had to ask for the door back, which I got a month later.

Yes, as I mentioned, my dad was a joiner but also a mad McGarvey, so his methods where a tad unconventional, although they did work. Oh, how he drove my twin and me crazy when, as teenagers, we liked our lie-in sat the weekend. He would often put the hoover on outside our room or start mowing the lawn at 'stupid o'clock' (well, probably 10am which is 'stupid o'clock' to a teenager!) and then sing to the radio at the top of his voice. The sign on the kitchen door saying 'Breakfast' served between 7 and 10am was now closed because we were too late, was annoying for a pair of stroppy teens. Oh, how David and I wanted to emancipate our dad when one Saturday, Granny Ann was sick and in bed (yes, one time we remember that she actually took to her bed).

Daddy once had a list of groceries and presented it to us with the dreaded cream, granny-looking shopping trolley with wheels. We were told we had to go to the local Co-op five minutes from the house together and use the trolley to bring the groceries back. Oh, how we protested at the social suicide of having to walk the streets with this trolley on a Saturday! Seeing that our protests had fallen on deaf ears, we still laugh at how we overcame this injustice. David and I took turns to run ahead and make sure the coast was clear of our friends and then we would signal to the other who ran like the clappers with this dodgy trolley. We did the quickest supermarket sweep when we got there and the same tactics were activated on the way home. Albeit was a little harder with a full shopping trolley to run fast. With our dignity and reputation at stake we gave it our all and oh, how we high-fived when we made it home unseen by our friends. I still remember that cream trolley to this day and it makes me giggle at our escapades to get there and back unseen.

We loved when he told us stories of his dad's parenting that was just as mad as his, that I have mentioned before, with the brothers fighting over a shared bike. You'll also remember the story of the alarm clock in the Daddies Are Really Superheroes in Disguise chapter – so you'll understand where his mad genes came from!

I don't know when it really happens – probably when you leave the nest and head to university. For me, that's when my parents were seen in a new light. They become more friends as well as your parents. You actually get to a point where you don't mind being seen with them in public. We will all admit to ducking and diving as awkward teens when seen with parents by our peers at some point. Or was that just me? Eek! You like to keep in touch because you want to, not because you feel you have to. You go through a phase of even socialising with them – shock horror – and enjoy it. Yes, in a way they are still your superhero and wing woman but on a more equal level. Yes, we may be grown-ups now but we can still call on them for help, especially DIY skills.

I remember when we bought our home and dad came to help us move in. He looked around and asked, "Did you view this with your eyes closed?" and then we both laughed as he tried to calm my panic by rhyming off about how, by doing this bit of work, etc, that he and Law would have the place sorted. Fast forward ten-plus years later we are nearly there. I recently made a phone-a-friend call to help me dodge an IKEA disaster assembly and dodge a divorce when my hubby came home, so we still need our superheroes. Our wing women are still needed, even as adults. Sometimes juggling work, children and life is hard and meltdowns occur. In times of crisis, Granny Ann and her corned beef sandwiches and Jamie Dodgers are the best comfort.

In the last few years I have really begun to appreciate their presence. When we lost Law's mum at fifty-nine – far too young – we saw how fragile life is. I saw first-hand how a family implodes emotionally and physically when they lose one of their parents. I remember to this day Law's dad saying when his mum passed away 'the powerhouse is gone' or words to that effect, and I remember getting that. Your mum really is the anchor, the nerve centre of the family for sure. This, again, was reiterated to me when at a funeral of a family friend when I overheard a man comforting the daughter and stating that 'this is the hardest loss, the mother leaving'. That again struck a chord as an elderly man who seemed to be saying this from his own experience of losing his mother figure said it. Over the last few years and then recently I have witnessed how a few close friends have gone through the sad loss of a parent. This is where it got me thinking recently that your dad, your superhero and your mum, your wing woman whom for most of your life is seen as infallible is then not there. Be this through an illness that they do not recover from or suddenly falling unwell and passing on – really, the solo flight of your superhero/wing woman. The one-way ticket with no return that you cannot accompany them on must be the hardest, scariest and loneliest journey to travel. I gained a good friend through a conversation with her on her journey through grief and with the help of an Oreo. I saw her in a different light as she talked of her dad and her loss but also of the memories she shared of him which showed that, really, even though they leave, that, in our hearts, they always will remain.

I think, as I have said to friends that have lost parents, what touches us all at these times is that this is indeed a universal loss that we all know will come to our doors and that we all dread. We feel the pain of our friend's loss as we can have empathy and try and understand. Again, that is why I love the tradition of the Irish wake. In the wakes that I have been to, what often touched me was how in a room full of family and sadness that it was often sprinkled with laughter; yes, tears but also of laughter. That people come to pay respects and offer support. In the time when their hearts are breaking the doors are open and, like a warm hug, people come bearing food and stories of their loved ones. Either stories the family did not know of a generous act, kindnesses shown by their parent towards others or funny anecdotes. I have seen how these stories help heal and warm their hearts. That the parent they held so highly was too revered by others. Now, I am glad in a way that the tradition of having the deceased sat in an armchair has changed to a coffin. For as much as I love my parents, the thought of them sitting in an armchair in their deceased state is not my cup of tea (that really was a mad Irish tradition).

Life is indeed precious and our parents are very precious commodities. Sometimes we forget, as I have said, with our busy lives to keep in touch. I know that families are often scattered all over the globe these days but technology is still the key. It takes five minutes to Skype, ring and just re-connect with your superhero and wing woman. To say hi, chat about nothing and just enjoy the conversation. Those that have lost would love this gift as I remember there are no telephones to heaven so live, laugh and love in the present as the past is gone and the future is not guaranteed. This may be a bit deep but sometimes we need to appreciate what is here before it's gone. Now, go pick a fight or have a vent with your superhero/wing woman and then have a cuppa and corned beef sandwich and all will be well.

Work-Life Balance - The Struggle is Real But Worth it

Today I am writing on my deck as it's not raining; having found a window where I am off work, Hannah is playing outside, as it's sunny – yes, sunny in Ireland – it can happen. Daddy bear is in his cave sleeping off a night duty. It has indeed been a hectic several weeks since our superhero/princess turned six on June 21st (where have the years gone?)

This year our annual leave was jam-packed – not planned that way initially – but that's how it turned out. We had a camping break booked and the concert was a birthday present, albeit the unexpected Spanish holiday was last-minute and I will explain later. One of my best friends said we were like the Kardashians with our gallivanting, but really, it was the Lidl version. We spent a fabulous week in Spain that was hot due to a heat wave but we coped well under the circumstances. This year we saw especially how quickly the dear daughter can grow and it was a mixed blessing. Last year on holidays Hannah was a bit shy about the fabulous creation that is kids' club. One day she lasted an hour before being brought back to us as she missed us. This year, however, she became a big six and it was a big change. Her first question when we were booking was, 'Is there a kids' club?' Her first quest on arrival was to find out the timetable for the kids' club and where it was situated.

Now, I know that kids' clubs are kind of a Marmite thing for parents, some think they are amazing and the best invention ever (we are included in this group) although the other group of parents are not so enamoured and feel a slight tightness in their chest at the thought of leaving their precious minions with strangers, especially in a different country. We were probably of that thinking until we really looked into it as Hannah got older and we were more financially stable to travel more and so became aware of these clubs. We think they are fabulous! For all the family – 'Why?' you may ask. Well, it's not so that we can 'pam' her off for a few hours and have peace (although that is a bonus if am being honest) the main reason we became interested is when we first observed them in action when around the pool, especially when Hannah was four. Firstly, what struck us the most was how safe it seemed; the employees were very vigilant, the kids were looked after well and supervised closely. Secondly, all the kids seemed to love it and loved the staff; we watched how they smiled and waved excitedly when they marched happily past their parents during club activities. We also watched how these clubs transfixed Hannah as they marched past in their little procession, often face-painted and singing wee songs. She became curious and asked if she could go. Law and I looked horrified at each other as, at that time, we were in the camp of chest tightening at the thought of leaving her with a group of strangers, especially when this group barely spoke English. We were in a very Spanish resort, not touristy and, coupled with the memory of the scary stories of kids abroad being abducted, we were initially not happy about trying it if we were honest.

Then we wised up and thought perhaps Hannah was being denied a chance to go and have fun with kids her age, of a different culture and in a safe environment because of our fears and insecurities. Now that Dylon didn't holiday with us any more she was on her own unless there were kids her age at the pool. Yes, we couldn't deny that awful things had been reported of abductions of children in foreign countries but that they occurred in this crazy world we live in anyway. Those bad things happen all over, whether on holidays or not, and attending a kids' club wouldn't change that. We realised if we checked it out and we did like it then we were really denying her a fun experience due to our fears if it all seemed safe and above-board.

Now, that's not to say that when we left her that first day we didn't watch from a safe distance and 'gleek' in the window a lot. She also took a while to settle and, as I said, the first day only lasted an hour and she came back although by the end of the week she was fully involved and, even though she was the only English-speaking child, she got on fabulously. This proves that kids can overcome all barriers in the world of play. She even took part in a show at the end of the week and was a little minion singing songs in Spanish proudly that she may not have known the meaning of (neither did we) but that she sang proudly and had the best fun. From then on our love of kids' club grew and has flourished ever since.

This year was no exception and I was able to read a book and relax knowing Hannah was having fun just metres away from us. I know this as I signed her in, walked out the gate and pulled my sun lounger right outside and relaxed. Yes, the staff looked a bit amused when I first did this but then they became used to it and often conversed with me over the gate. I think I started a craze too as other parents adopted our plan. The kids' club got more kiddies and the parents parked their sun loungers beside the kids' clubs and could relax, read a book or sunbathe knowing their precious minions were safe and close by. This year, because of kids' club, Hannah got to experience the water mat and overcame her fear by conquering it and running on it alone, all thanks to encouragement of the staff in kids' club. She also attended her first foam party, a party that neither of her parents even experienced growing up. Hannah also shared her joy at another baby tooth falling out and everyone in the club cheered. When we holidayed in Bundoran in the south of Ireland, the kids' club was just as fabulous as our foreign club and had activities going on from 9am until late. Hannah loved it. Again, we had researched it before we had gone and it was the top reason for selecting this hotel. Hannah once more had the timetable given to her directly on check-in with crayons and a wee pack. This we thought was a great touch and she felt so grown-up getting something especially for her. We stayed two days there and Hannah was more inclined to spend time at the mini club engaging in the activities there than with us. When we had dinner she refused dessert (never does this happen) because she was eager to get back to her friends at the club. She also attended the DVD and hot chocolate evening at 9pm, so we were able to relax with a nightcap knowing she was safe and not far from us.

I even got to have a hot stone massage and her daddy had a wee quiet pint while she attended an activity with the club. Now, hot stone massages I would definitely recommend to mad mammies, stressed-out ladies and actually all humans.

I can't get my hubby to try it yet which puzzles me when he gets sport massages that are not relaxing, but the thought of lying having a relaxing massage fills him with horror (men are indeed a strange species). We think these clubs enhance the family holiday for all so it's a win-win, really. I would encourage all parents out there to give these clubs a try. Yes, research the club attached to your hotel; the Internet is great for this and publishes reviews for you to see.

When our estranged stepson, Dylon, was wee (he is going through the chapter of being eighteen and therefore an adult, apparently knowing all there is to know about life and parents – not so cool – but we have hope that this chapter will soon close). Teenagers are indeed strange and wonderful creatures. I am dreading Hannah entering them, eugh... When he was wee, most of our holidays were in beautiful Ireland, more so due to the fact we had just bought a house, Law was afraid of flying and didn't overcome that fear until we got married and I was back doing my nurse training, so our disposable income was not what it is now.

Even though our budget was not what it is now we still had fun camping and having a few nights in hotels up and down the country and day trips away. Kids' club was not that big a trend then and, to be honest, the hubby at the time enjoyed most of what Dylon did such as fishing and playing football that, really, he had another kid with him to play (probably in mental age too if I am honest). We have pictures of Dylon catching his first fish, playing in the sea and camping – all still evoke happy memories. It still makes me laugh the time we camped at Achill Island when he was ten, as the hubby was still fighting to put up the tent, Dylon declared he was off to play with his friends. The hubby and I looked at each other in disbelief at the fact we had only just landed and he was off networking already. That was also the year he asked to borrow his dad's hair wax and we knew then that he was on the cusp of the dreaded teenage years, ha!

The last time we went camping Hannah was just turning two – her first camping trip and Dylon's last. That was the year he wouldn't play kick about with Law as being fourteen was hard enough without being seen playing footie with your dad in a campsite where there were other teenagers watching. I remember laughing as Law tried to fathom why he could possibly be embarrassing as he was a young dad, having had Dylon when he was twenty-two. I explained to him no matter if you are a cool dad, young dad or rock star, all dads are embarrassing when you're fourteen. This was also the first holiday we didn't have to bribe him to shower, another realisation the family holidays where coming to an end. When Hannah was four we visited Euro Disney and Dylon, at first, said, 'No way 'and then, 'OK'. Peppa Pig World the year before was a definite no from him and he didn't change his mind on that which we kind of understood. Now he was fifteen and I get that the idea of Disney with your family, especially for a boy, would be horrifying initially. I think, however, that on the whole he did enjoy it – a fact I think he would refute. You see, when you get to Disney you realise that it really isn't for kids but all ages. It was full of couples, groups of young people all mixed with families and their star struck toddlers running around after their favourite characters for that desired photo. We have photos of Hannah with her favourite princess and all the Disney gang. I still remember her wee expressions when we had dinner and the Disney crew came round the tables to say 'Hi'. We also have a picture of Dylon being chatted up by

Minnie Mouse and he took it well for being a teenager. I also love the family picture that we had taken when a kind waitress offered to take a picture, much to the horror of Dylon. It was etched all over his face in that picture – having a family picture taken in public was sooo not cool for him.

We also went camping on our annual leave this year to a wee gem of a place in Creeslough that is great and safe for kids. We did a few nights in the pods and even had the unexpected last-minute planned arrival of one of my best mad mammy friends to join in the experience. Now, 'clamping' is great as you get all the fun out of camping but you get a warm shelter and a soft bed at the end of the night although the following week we returned and did the old-fashioned camping in a tent we have from when Hannah was two and only used a handful of times since we fell in love with the pods. This tent was resurrected from its home under our stairs and, I have to say that experiencing life in a proper tent was not so bad, especially with the invention of airbeds that make it so much more bearable. Now, those of you who remember the fun of the summer camps in our youths will remember that wooden floors and sleeping bags were not so comfy although I think youth was on our side and didn't trouble our backs as much as it would being adults. Our camping trips also made me think fondly of the times we camped out in our back gardens and at the top of our streets as teenagers in not-so waterproof tents without airbeds but it was fun.

This trip with Hannah and my fellow mad mammy's kids was just as fun but the kids had the added bonus of a park in the middle of the camp to occupy them and, even when the weather turned rainy, a waterproof jacket and boots kept them going and didn't dampen their spirits. A few flashlights thrown in when dusk turned and they were occupied for ages playing hide-and-seek. Even mad Max, the youngest sibling on the trip who was on his debut camping trip, enjoyed the fun. He seemed mesmerised by everyone sleeping on the ground in a big colourful tent and, more importantly, that by the help of a big fire, the BBQ, he got fed as well, so he was happy. The kids loved the marshmallows being roasted on sticks, something that we never did as kids and probably introduced more now by our knowledge from American television programmes. They were yum except for Law who of course didn't like them (he is an anomaly!)

I still think that there is nothing more lovely as sitting round a fire pit (except when smoke wafts in your eyes, ha!) in good company. Knowing the kids are tucked up in their tents, sharing a wee 'vino' and enjoying the 'craic' while tucking into a BBQ, all delight as a few of life's cheap and cheerful pleasures. Having nice weather and trusty parka jackets when the chills of the nights set in are also good – it is Ireland and you have to be prepared.

We also got a sneaky wee concert night away in the middle of this, Hannah-free, which was fun to socialise as adults, even better when we collided with other adult friends and drank in the day and danced the night away in concert like it was 1999.

When reality bit and we both returned to work I reflected on our holiday and, even though it ended up jam-packed, we had a ball. As I said, the holiday to Spain was last-minute and happened as I decided when the seed was planted by my beloved to book a wee break in the sun instead rather than forgo my savings for new house blinds and. I am happy that I did as, really, the blinds were more for aesthetic accessorising purposes and will be purchased at a later date, unless Law plants another seed.

Time out and holidays, I think, are important for everyone, especially in this crazy world we live in. Most couples work hard and barely get time to wind down and chat properly in the madness of a working week, therefore planning regular breaks abroad or just exploring your own country is vital for your relationship. I have a friend who has discovered the beauty of travelling alone and gained great friends along the way. I have seen how she has grown in confidence, knowledge and her amount of freckles in doing so. We as well, as am sure many of her friends have benefited too, have booked trips through her sharing pictures, accommodation details and stories of her adventures.

Young people use the phrase YOLO a lot these days. It means you only live once. I think this is a great phrase. Lots of people plan for rainy days and put things off till tomorrow, always mañana (Spanish for tomorrow, I learned this on my trips). I disagree with this, as we should live in the moment no matter what our budget. What is important is getting away from the mundane same old routine of home – that is important. By having a different environment you are not distracted, your brain switches off and doesn't feel the need to do some cleaning, wash the car, etc. It is out of sight, therefore out of mind. It is then that you can re-charge, re-connect with each other, de-stress yourself and have a bit of escapism. That is why it is called a holiday. The meaning of which includes 'an extended period of leisure and recreation especially one spent away from home and travelling...'

How many of you have used a break from work and spent most of it at home and not even ventured outside the door? Perhaps busy doing house renovations, etc. Yes, all important tasks but when you do it for your entire holidays and nothing else is planned you feel cheated when you return to reality. At least I do and you would also feel less re-charged as you have not used your time away doing something fun and relaxing. Work–life balance is a struggle but worth it.

I say to you all out there – single, consciously happily coupling or mad mammies/daddies – make sure you use your time off wisely. Plan or maybe book a last-minute break like we did and forgo your house blinds. Do something fun whether abroad or near. Try camping or glamping, both of which are fun for all. No matter what your budget escape from the norm, even for the day – pack your car with a picnic, always remembering your waterproofs, especially in Ireland, ha! Take in the beauty of the world we live in. Cheesy as it sounds, remember to smell the roses and engage with your family and friends. Enjoy their company or not when you realise why you don't see them as often. A bit awkward if that person's your partner though. My beloved and I have rarely had a bad word exchanged on holiday – amazing for us. Of course, we had niggles each day but that is the norm. Enjoy the sunsets, BBQ, vino, friendly catch-ups and may the kiddie meltdowns, couple meltdowns or car/plane/train delays, be few and far between during your holiday period.

Solo Journey to Sole Island

Those that know me well, especially my work colleagues in the last year, have heard me harp on about my fascination around Lough Derg. I talked about it all last summer and then chickened out as no one would come on the journey with me, or those that were going to didn't match up with my time off to do it. To be honest, I think I was secretly glad, as even though I was fascinated by it I was also a little bit wary of the challenge. I am also not a fan of feet (my own are painted all year round as I feel they need a lot of help to look prettier) so the thought of being in the presence of many feet, many that might not be painted, did make me queasy.

Lough Derg to those that are not familiar is an island in County Donegal that is surrounded by legends of what occurred on it. This could be a blog in itself, so I will share the legend of St Patrick's Purgatory but if, like me, you are a nerd for knowledge, research this yourself and you will be enthralled by the mystery surrounding this island. Obviously, as I have mentioned before, the nerd in me soaked up all I could find about the place in the week before I went. In the words of Margaret Fuller: 'If you have knowledge, let others light their candles in it'. I am sharing my snippets of this island with you – do with the knowledge what you wish, ha!

The word Derg comes from the Irish word Derg that means red and reflects the staining effect of the surrounding bog land. Legend states that the colour of the water occurred as the result of St Patrick slaying the dragon that had terrorised the people. Legend also states that Christ showed St Patrick a cave, or some would describe as a pit, on Station Island on Lough Derg that was the entrance to purgatory. This fact is clearly shown on texts from 1185 and can be seen on maps from all over Europe from as early as the 15th century. It is also recorded as the only Irish site on Martin Behaim's world map of 1492. Pilgrims have been coming for almost fifteen hundred years, beginning their three-day pilgrimage from the start of June until August 13th when it finishes for the year. Apparently, in the past, it lasted nine days. Now, that to me would be a real challenge but not one I would have wished to undertake – three days gave me enough insight. It entails three days of fasting, praying and depriving yourself of sleep while walking barefoot around the station beds (why they are called beds is beyond me as they are rough, upturned stones, at places very slippery and not a soft bouncy cushion bit to be had…) They are believed to have been the remains of monastic huts. It is open to all religions as long as you are older that fifteen years of age, in good health and able to kneel and walk unaided. Many a famous writer or poet throughout time have come here, the likes of Seán Ó'Faoláin and Patrick Kavanagh. Our very own Seamus Heaney did a collection of poems around Station Island and his experiences there.

Now that I have given you a bit of history around this island I am eager to share my experience of my pilgrimage. The story begins on me actually physically getting to the boat and, anyone who knows me will tell you that my geography/ navigation skills are not very good; actually, they are shocking and I own up to it, ha. I think my twin was given the geography gene and I got nothing, only the ability to chat and ask for help. At university it took me months to successfully visit my friend's halls on the bus even though the route was straight and, to everyone else, idiot proof. I was often the last person sitting on the bus and having to be transferred to another bus by the driver as I had ended up at the depot. I know, the shame... I once had to ring my dad on an actual payphone, as mobiles were not as available then, to ask for directions around Manchester when I had got lost again... In hindsight, I don't know how my parents coped having me in another country with a geography gene deficit. I must have driven them mad with worry. Actually, I probably still do.

In the age of technology I was a bit more confident setting off on my solo journey as I had my trusty satnav on my mobile so I was confident that this would be easy peasy... As I was approaching the old bridge just five minutes into my journey, I observed traffic jams and police presence everywhere. After a frantic call to the hubby I calmed down. I hollered to a police officer for information and was happy to know that it was all good, just parades going on and the traffic would begin flowing shortly. A short time later I had music blaring, open roads and my satnav was behaving. I relaxed and looked forward to beginning my solo pilgrimage where I would be away from the TV, phones (when not experiencing a panic) and stresses of daily life to spend time on my own, clearing my head. In no time I spied a sign for Lough Derg and was on schedule. The satnav lady spoke and told me to take the next left and I did so confidently, feeling relieved that I was nearing my destination. Did I notice that the road was getting narrower and more off-road looking? Um, maybe, but I was on a high and did not think on it. That was until I saw a locked farm gate ahead and realised, eugh... I was in the wrong place. Now, as I was still brimming with confidence I didn't panic. I worked out that I would just turn and get back on the normal road and it would be fine. That was fine in my head but in reality it was not so easy. The road was so narrow that three-point turn moves were not an option. The road surface was muddy and, on one attempt, a crazy, dodgy sound had me out of the car inspecting. Yup, not good; I had pulled something off my car and it was lying in the middle of the road. Now, I am not a mechanic and, superficially, it looked fine and, as I have had bumps in the past that have knocked bits off under my car (car park in Altnagelvin Area Hospital where I hugged the kerb, it still gives me nightmares) I decided to put the piece in the boot and think about that after I got out of this madness. My reversing skills also let me down and after one more try I ended up with the back of the car in a ditch. My gearbox didn't seem to be working and I began to panic. It didn't help that my daughter's car seat was sitting on the passenger seat next to me and the Batman face on it was staring at me blankly. I admit I did shout at it saying he was some help and it was not the first time he had let me down (yup, I admit it, I shout at inanimate objects often especially when, like her seat, they have a superhero face on them).

In times of panic you ring for help, right? So, I rang my hubby and vented my situation to him. Yes, in my head while waiting for him to answer I was calm and ready to divulge my situation in that manner although, on answering, I turned into a frustrated psycho Annie. It didn't help when my beloved asked where I was and I didn't know, which further made me lose it. told him if he had driven me this would have never happened, but not to worry as I would sort it myself before I hung up, feeling like a crazy person. For a few seconds I didn't know whether to cry or get out and do a Basil Fawlty moment – grab a branch and hit my car. The logical side won and I calmly stepped out of my car, grabbed my raincoat as of course it had started to rain (again, I did lose my cool and threw my hands up in the air shouting, 'Really, God? I am trying to get to Lough Derg, give me a break!') I then composed myself and headed in the direction of a house that I had passed on up the road, taking heed of my hubby's advice to go and ask for help. In my mind, at this stage, I had resigned myself to the fact that I would not make a boat and this made me sad then annoyed as my damn phone's satnav kept piping up that I was near my destination (yes, I did call that satnav lady a few choice words on my muddy trip up the road for help). Finally, I found the house and, when passing a small window, I found a man staring back at me, probably thinking *Who is this crazy in waterproofs and smiling manically at me mouthing that she needs help?*

He opened the door and I was confronted by a typically wee old Irish man who appeared to live on his own and, from my quick observation of his home, seemed to have kept everything he had ever owned in his life. A typical wee hoarder but my plight quickly brought me back to reality so, after explaining my trouble he grabbed his coat and we were setting off down the road in his wee white van telling me that my car must be at Tommy's field. My hubby rang as we were travelling and I explained that I had help and was on my way back. My hubby asked who the man was and he told me he was Francey McGrath and, in turn, I told my hubby (in hindsight I now know that he wanted a name to track me if I ended up being murdered and not returning from the trip). Francey turned out to be a sweet man who expertly reversed my car up the windy land in no time and told me the car was probably fine, just cosmetic damage to the car. He told me could still make the boat as it was only five minutes down the road. I was so delighted I hugged him and told him he was a 'dote'. He laughed and told me to head on and could he have a kiss for his help. Now, at that moment I thought Jeeze, mister, you're chancing your arm but because I was so grateful I gave him a wee peck and sure, it might have given him a wee lift, as he probably doesn't see many people from day-to-day. I did chuckle as I drove off although thinking that men are all the same no matter what their age.

Five minutes' drive later and there it was, the big sign for Lough Derg. I parked at the bottom of the car park and for few seconds I sat there contemplating should I go or should I just head home? as I was exhausted already from my trip here. When I opened my eyes I saw a man getting out of a car and coming towards mine. For a split second I thought Jeeze, can I not have a minute to myself, Lord, are you kidding me? The man approached the window and, on pushing the button, he asked if I knew when the boat was leaving or whether he had he missed it. I explained to him that this was my first time too but that if he made his way to reception to pay that I was sure they would tell him. He turned to me at this point, confused, and said 'You have to pay?' This made me laugh out loud and I explained that it was sixty euros, so he scurried off to his car to see what money he had. I watched from my car as he seemed to count his money and so I gathered my stuff ready to go too. When I was walking to reception I shouted to ask him if he had enough. He replied back that he only had fifty-five euros and he seemed deflated, so I told him I would give him the other five. He nearly skipped down to me. He thanked me and told me he would pay me back. I told him to wise up, just to say a wee prayer for me as I thought I would need it, ha!

I headed to reception, paid my money and the girl asked for an emergency contact name and number. I told her the details were in my mobile in my car and I didn't know the details off by heart. I then had to run to the far end of car park to find the number. I had no pen so improvised using nail varnish on paper. I then ran back and explained to the girl about the nail varnish through deep breathing – they both laughed. I had missed the boat but the receptionist booked me onto the next. I asked to use the toilet as I'd spied the disabled on the way and ran in there. I then proceeded to get self-locked in the toilet; again, I shout loudly to the big man, 'seriously' struggle with the lock, bang against it and finally fall out of it. I see the boat arriving at the dock and throw my frazzled body down the hill, all the while my inner voice is calling out, 'Go home, you eejit, don't go – you have been through enough this morning'. I ignore that voice although I do find it hard not to turn and run, but I stepped onto the boat, sank into a plastic chair and wondered what on earth I was letting myself in for.

There was only myself, a couple, two girls and a lone ranger on the boat. We soon arrived at our location, departed the boat and ushered up to reception to be shown our dorms and begin our pilgrimage. I got that queasy feeling you get when you don't know what is in front of you and are a wee bit excited but a wee bit terrified all at the same time. I walked up three flights of stairs to find my room and, on entering my room, I was faced with two bunk beds, a few shelves for clothes and a sink in the middle with only a cold water tap. I sank down on the bed (that was more like a wide bench) and let out a nervous giggle. The set-up reminded me of the set of the programme Prisoner: Cell Block H. The walls were thin partition walls with gaps at the bottom and top. There were no lights in the rooms, just a strip of lights in the corridor that shone a small amount on the bed area. I figured that, as I wouldn't be in the dorm much I observed it was clean and so got over it. I had been given advice from many before coming such as to make my bed up on the first day so that it was ready for me to fall into after my 36hr vigil of no sleep. It also prevents fights with duvet covers when you're in a zombie state. I robotically did this and then removed my shoes and socks and headed down to the unknown to try and work out what to do.

I walk towards the basilica building (the main chapel) and observed a sea of people, all barefoot like me, wandering around with rosary beads in their hands and all in their own wee worlds of prayer. I have to admit I did have thoughts of Dear Lord, what am I doing here? These people must be mad, then I thought Eek! I must be mad too as I am here with them and then I stifled a giggle and told myself to behave. I am directed to a cloakroom where I can leave my bag with water and extra layers of clothes for later as you cannot go up again as they lock the dorms when vigil begins. This again made me giggle as I thought This is madness and I have come here voluntarily!

Whilst I was busy putting my bag away and getting my water, I overheard a girl chatting to two men and I observed that she seemed to be a pro at this. My inner voice advised me,

'Get to know her, she will help', so I piped up, "Hello," popped my head round the coat rails and admitted that this was my first time and could anyone advise me on what to do. Thankfully, my first impression of the girl was right. She automatically took me under her wing and told me she was beginning her second station so would show me the ropes. What she had said meant nothing to me at that point but I was thankful she was willing to help me and I followed her gratefully. I asked her if she had she done this many times and she said that this was her fifth time – I was amazed. She said she couldn't believe I had come on my own for the first time and that I was brave to do so. I laughed and replied, 'Brave or foolish?' and we both chuckled. She handed me a leaflet that set out what you do and explained that there are certain actions which might make me feel a bit foolish but she was sure that everyone would be doing the same so just to go with the flow.

I confide in her that my first impression is that this place is a little bit mad and she reassures me this is normal but that it becomes quite meditative as you go along as you will get something from it. Armed with my leaflet and advice from Aileen (that was her name, Aileen Murphy, my station starter) she told me to do it at my own pace and she would catch up with me as she was not as fit this time. I walked around the basilica building trying to navigate my rosary beads to count the prayers. Aileen helped me remember how to use them. I know she was thinking Are you really a Catholic? (I remembered the jest of it, I just needed to confirm it) although on my second circle of the building I was twiddling with the crucifix and it fell off. Yes, I am in the middle of doing a pilgrimage and I break my rosary beads. I scanned the ground frantically but could see nothing. I couldn't ask people to help as I felt shame that I had lost the crucifix so I spent the next circle apologising in prayer about the crucifix, for being the worst pilgrim ever and praying that I find it. I don't, however, and make amends with myself that it was not my fault, just faulty beads, and continue onto the beds. I have described earlier that these beds are circles of stones that are upturned and sharp and at times slippery. Rumours have it that the priests sharpen them for the beginning of the pilgrimages.

At this point I am getting into it and, as you are busy reciting the different prayers in your head, you do seem to go into a meditative state – you clear your head of everything, as you are busy concentrating on prayer and it feels good. You are aware of others around you but you don't care, you are consumed in your own wee journey, as are they. You share a smile if you catch their eye; a hand is held out if you stumble and you slowly make your way around the beds until you come to the water's edge – this became my favourite part of the stations. I have to admit this was partly because I knew I was near the end but also because of the scenery – as you knelt in prayer it was so beautiful. You overlooked the calm waters and you did get a sense of peace. I have to admit that you do get transfixed so much so, that I did lose count in my prayers as my rosary beads were hidden in shame after losing the crucifix and I was using fingers to count. I did once rely on the person beside me to help gauge when I was ready to move on as they had knelt shortly after me.

Now, the vigil part was interesting for me as, being a nurse and having done night duty, I was confident I could cope with this part, no problem. What I hadn't factored in was that by that stage I hadn't eaten much, only wheaten bread and black tea so I was not only tired from my eventful journey but also tired from the three stations I had completed that, in turn, it took at least one hour to complete. So, by 4am I had walked for several hours praying and was sleep deprived and cold. I was very cold again. I had been warned to bring layers for the night and I was well layered, but being barefooted you still feel the cold in a weird sense right to the bone.

Now, all you nurses out there will know the feeling when you hit the wall on night duty as you struggle to stay alert and deal with documents at stupid o'clock, you wonder What am I doing with my life? How did I end up here when I should be sleeping like normal people? Then you sometimes become giddy and high as you approach the end of the shift and the world is OK again and all is well. Well, on this pilgrimage I hit that wall at around 4am as I wandered around the chapel, praying and chanting with the other 120 people, kneeling and walking in a daze at times. At one point I noted that the caller leading us in prayer was now speaking in Irish and, for a split second, I thought I was the only one hearing this. Was I experiencing auditory hallucinations? Eek. A quick scan and an eager ear to the crowd and I realised that everyone was now speaking in Irish and I wasn't so freaked out although I had to stifle a giggle at my mad thoughts.

As I knelt I observed all the others layered up with hats, scarves, gloves and all barefooted as me. I saw some nodding off as they walked and I giggled as we all walked more slowly and attempted to bag a seat at the padded benches at the front for a bit of comfort to our battered knees from the kneeling on rocks throughout the day. Obviously it was done in a passive way but it did remind me of the sunbed dashes you see on holidays, but this was for a padded knee bench. The cushioned feeling against your wee knees for that short time was bliss though. It was on one of these kneeling sessions where I failed to bag a soft bench and slid into a hard, wooden one, something weird happened. I glanced down at the bench and there I saw a crucifix. Now, I know that it was stupid o'clock and as I had not eaten or slept in a while I feared I was now visually hallucinating. I discreetly reached out and grabbed it. Yes, it was real and I pulled my hidden rosary beads out of my pocket and couldn't believe that it was indeed the cross from my beads. I was quickly alerted to start walking again by the other pilgrims and walked the last of the station holding my rosary beads and cross tightly in my hand. I thought this through and acknowledged that obviously someone had found the cross and left it on the bench in the chapel. The peculiar part was that the chapel is huge and the bench it was left on was not one I would have made my way to willingly, only that I had to kneel. Sat there in my tired stupor, I came across it.

The morning station ended with an amazing sunset over the lake and a stillness that was so breathtakingly lovely. A pilgrim remarked that it couldn't get much better than this. I thought Oh, but if we were sitting on a yacht out there with a cold vino that would be much better. I realised then that my 'internal' voice had let me down and I turned to stare at the group beside me who had all burst out laughing and appeared to agree with looks that said 'yes, that does sound better', but for now we would take in the view.

The second day is tough as you have completed your stations and you just have to stay awake until 10pm. You are allowed as much water or Lough Derg soup if you're brave (hot water with salt and pepper). I took a sip and decided to stick with hot and cold water instead. I was lucky that the weather was lovely and the sun was out. Even so, I remained layered up as, because you are sleep deprived and fasting, you feel the cold more and you are also barefoot, don't forget. I sat at different seats dotted around the island and with my sunglasses on I let the sun warm my bones and tired feet. It was the most at peace I had felt. You do confession in the morning and, even though since losing our son Jacob I had fallen out with God (he was still on my pending friend list, I hadn't blocked him totally) after speaking with the priest I felt a sense of peace. Now, I am no 'Holy Joe', as the Derry slang would say, but after chatting with the priest I felt a sense of contentment. I had told him I had come here on a whim. He asked if I had known what I would endure here and I replied that I did. He then said something that stuck with me; he said, 'Well, if you knew how hard this was going to be I don't think it was on a whim you came', but that I was meant to come. I discussed a few things with him that I needed clarity on and he helped me see that whatever I decided regarding my issues he felt my time here would leave me with a sense of contentment. Whatever I worked out I would feel at ease with it, knowing I had done my best.

This all resonated with me and as that day unfolded I let the sun envelop me and kept my mind clear. I engaged with random pilgrims as they rested and chatted. I gained encouragement from them when tiredness enveloped my body and I wanted to lie on the ground and sleep. There were lots of laughs as they told stories related to what their families thought of their trips to the island, etc. They told me amusing stories of a girl who had turned up with her bathing suit and asked where the swimming facilities were. I found that many had come more than once, some twenty or thirty times; they said something always seemed to call them back. Some there, like me, where not very holy but believed in something and always felt re-charged after taking part in a pilgrimage. They loved escaping from the world of work, kids, relationships and technology and just concentrating on them. They all acknowledged that it was like meditation. I overheard a few confiding that they didn't tell their workmates or friends of their visit. They felt that they wouldn't understand or think they were weird 'Holy Joes'. This made me giggle but also a bit sad. I guess that it is ignorance that makes people afraid to admit it. I, on the other hand, told everyone I was going, more so that I couldn't back out. I do feel this place deserves to be spoken of. It is not somewhere you would force someone to go but I think it is a place that draws you to it and if you go with it, emerge yourself into it fully – you will find an inner peace and contentment that I can't describe. The island is beautiful and the views are spectacular.

The night vigil that ended with us heading to bed was like Christmas Eve. You were so tired it was hard to focus on the words as you knew bed would be coming soon. I sat there with a girl, Aiobhan, who had been many times and we sat deliberately at the back so we could rush to bed first. The priest was saying the Gospel and I heard the name Jacob and heaven's gate and my heart leapt. On return I did my research and learned that it was the story of Jacob's dream at Bethal. Now, there are many stories in the Bible but it just made me tingle that on this pilgrimage it was the one with a Jacob mentioned – the name of my precious son born too soon. I couldn't help but get a warm feeling, even if it was just a coincidence or my starved state or sleep deprivation, I started reading more into it other than that it was a story in the Bible that just happened to mention Jacob. They also focused on the prodigal son. That also resonated with me as we had just welcomed our estranged teenager back into our home as he was finding his way in the crazy world of adulthood. He realised that parents/step-parents can help and are not the enemy.

When we were allowed to bed it really did feel like Christmas; we all scurried out the doors giving a nod to the new pilgrims whom were only just beginning their vigil and skipped off to bed. Sinking into that narrow bed was divine and after my body heated up I slept like a log until awakened by a warped version of Hi-de-hi! Picture a priest calling over a tannoy wishing us a good morning and calling us to chapel at 6.15am. I jumped out of bed despite the time, rested from my few hours' sleep. I was elated that today I was going home; I hadn't backed out, I had done it and it felt great. I did stifle a giggle when I passed the dorm next to me and was met with the two friends giving off about no lights in the dorm and how they couldn't get their makeup on.

On entering the chapel for the last time I observed the weary pilgrims who were tired and cold from their night vigil and felt a pang of sympathy for them. I decided to do my last station indoors as it was raining and I felt I didn't have to prove anything more to myself by doing it in the rain. You are allowed to choose on the last day and many had decided, like me, to end our pilgrimage inside. It was my last station and I had a feeling of contentment. I finished blessing myself and wandered out and back down to collect my things and catch the ferry. I watched as the other pilgrims made their way around the beds and I got it – I got why people still come here year after year. Yes, there are some for whom their faith is so strong they do this naturally as part of their faith. The sight of some very elderly people kneeling and praying does sometimes make you want to help but then you see the determined faces and you know they are fine but if assistance is needed that they will ask. From the different mix of people I chatted with and from hearing their stories I realised that many, like me, just wanted time to reflect, re-charge, work out the madness in their lives and gain clarity and closure.

I came to this island on a whim although since returning home I agree with the priest that it probably wasn't a whim, it was something that I needed to do. On hearing of this island and the nerd in me researching it, it did in a weird way call me. I needed somewhere to reflect, empty my head, work out the madness and that I did. I came away with a sense of contentment that I have not felt ever. I felt a sense of peace that what will be will be. That I have given my all to certain parts of my life and that I can do no more. Obviously I have remained pleasantly mad but, sure, I wouldn't want to change that. I still have a geography deficit and as I had forgotten to turn my phone off in the car I arrived off the boat to my car and a dead mobile. Thankfully for me my fellow pilgrims' bus had broken-down (not so thankful for them) and I was able to get directions from them. So you see, God may not have given me the gift of direction but he gave me the gift of the gab to ask for help.

Lough Derg is tough but it is a challenge and an experience that I am glad I did. They say if you look back at the island on the way home that you will return. I didn't look back but I wouldn't rule out a return. We left that island a group of tired, hungry but elated people singing Hail Glorious Saint Patrick at the top of our voices and it felt good. This is also a part of the pilgrimage I loved – the singing. My beloved always makes fun of me for singing as if I think I am Beyoncé, but here I was able to sing like no one was watching. Why? It was acceptable and everyone else did too. Yes, some sounded tone-deaf, obviously not me, but we all sang our wee hearts out and it felt good. On reflection, I think my solo journey to Sole Island was a success – food for the soul but no mean feat/feet, boom boom!

Puppy Love

I am sitting writing this hiding from my family in my bedroom – yes, hiding! I have only just returned from a course and my head needs to de-clutter; the best therapy for this is writing. I can hear my beloved, the hubby, bellowing about him being the only one that empties bins around here, from the kitchen. In my mind I was debating all the chores I do that he never does but then I decided this is not a competition, so let his voice wash over me (mindfulness at play from course being activated). I also know if this was a competition I would obviously win...

In recent weeks we have had a new addition to the family; well two, actually, as my prodigal stepson has moved back in which is lovely except for his untidy habits, eating all my food and his awful-smelling football boots! He is now in training for working within a family again, being less self-absorbed, untidy, etc – all the usual nearly nineteen-year-old annoying habits. He, at present, is scoring an 'F' but is otherwise showing promise.

His returning home coincided with the arrival of our furry family member, Jessie, and he was present to collect her with Hannah and Law while I had been away walking barefoot around that island. Now, I have to say that I have never been a dog lover, never grew up with the urge to want or own one, probably because my parents were never overly keen to have one and always voiced that they never would. In our house we had what I class as low maintenance pets, which translates as boring. On the one hand we had the budgie that lived in the back hall that Granda Harry said Granny Ann had killed by not allowing it in the warm living-room. We had goldfish but, sure, not quite the same as a dog, you couldn't take them for a walk. You kind of got bored watching them swim after, say, five seconds... My hubby, on the other hand, grew up with dogs always being part of his family; his mum was a big dog lover and for years he had always badgered me to get one.

It wasn't until Hannah had left a note for God at her fairy door (yep, she loves to write like her mamma and includes God in her letters). On reading it, as obviously, I have to pretend to respond as God (being what you do for your six-year-old, right?) I learned that she was asking the man upstairs if she could please have a dog or baby or both – eek... After giggling at the letter with the hubby and as our journey to produce a sibling has not been plain sailing, the heart strings tugged a little harder and I decided that maybe a dog would be good for Hannah to grow up with. Of course, being the nerd I am I researched the benefits of children having pets and it showed a lot of positive reasons to do so. It stated that they help to nurture a well-adjusted human being, how they learned empathy and responsibility, etc. Her love for a dog was further impounded when she visited her

Auntie Caroline's dog, Monty, a gorgeous Cockapoo (well, I think that's what it is).

Then it seemed like in no time at all we were discussing the benefits, chatting to friends on their take on it and suddenly we had this little ball of white fluff, a Bichon Frise/Shih Tzu mix entering into our lives and forever changing it... It was a lovely return from Lough Derg to be greeted by another creature that would depend on me and I would have to clean up after it although at least she was cute!

A few months down the line and I can now liken her arrival to having your first baby. You kind of go into shock for a bit. A good shock though – you are in love with this cute, wee vulnerable creature; you watch it for hours as it shuffles about, sleeps and eats. You again liken it to when you were watching your growing child have excited clapping moments when she pees on her training mat and, well, when she does a number two that becomes a high-five/Mexican wave moment. You do again feel like the proud parent the first time you take her for a walk when a passer-by comments on her as if you had actually given birth to her yourself (or is that just me?)

I have to admit, I had that panic moment when I also had a baby – what I call an 'oh holey moley' moment. That time when you question everything in life. How can I be responsible for another person/animal? What was I thinking? Is this the worst decision ever? This is entirely my hubby's fault (or is this, again, just me?) although, once again, like a baby entering your life for the first time, a pet also integrates so easily that within a matter of weeks you can't imagine the house without them.

Now, don't get me wrong, the whole potty-training thing is not pleasant and I remember the first time the puppy travelled in the car with me and she pooped. I didn't panic as she was on a mat; that was until the smell hit me in a confined space and I nearly crashed the car attempting to pull over to breathe because of the stink. Who knew that a tiny dog could expel such a toxic smell? I remember the time she was sick on my fabric sofa! The not yet two-year-old was another shock to the system although I surprised myself by not freaking out and calmly removing the covers and washing them, praying they wouldn't shrink. You see, when you looked at the wee face it was the same as when you looked at a poorly child – you couldn't shout at them – they were sick, it wasn't their fault. I was pleased when my covers came out of the washer intact because on a positive note I found out they were machine-washable that day (before I was too afraid to try).

Becoming a puppy owner or mad dog mammy has also led us to the puppy obedience school, which has been a great success. As Hannah and I were new to this dog malarkey we thought it would benefit us so that she could learn to care for the dog in the right way and learn skills in a fun way. The couple that run the sessions are great. It is clear they have a passion for dogs and love to share their skills to help others care for dogs in a healthy and fun manner. The man, Robert, is very witty and says it how it is and is great with Hannah. His wife, Naomi, is also a great communicator and very approachable which makes you feel at ease to ask anything, even if it sounds stupid.

The first time I attended with Hannah it made me think it was probably how a child feels on their first day of school. We had all the puppies together in a shed, sitting beside their owners on leads, and all observing around them in an excited and nervous manner. We then had a socialisation bit where the dogs are slowly let off their leads a few at a time and they get to explore their surroundings and each other. Now, this is where it became funny. Some acted like the cool kids at school sauntering around not fazed, a few loitered around quite shy near their owners and, of course, we had the class clowns running around full of energy and confidence. Jessie interacted well after initially being shy although one poor pug got so excited that she literally shat herself – eek. This was met with an unfazed command by the trainers urging the owner to literally clean up the poop. The bad boy mop was wheeled in and in no time the lesson resumed albeit with a smelly aroma – I guess all part of 'Puppyville'). Since her first session she has graduated from the puppy class and is now nearing completion of the next class where, if she is successful, will receive a certificate – so exciting. She has mastered the sit, stay, down and re-call commands and is walking well on a lead, a skill we are as proud as punch of as if she was our kid at mainstream school.

A friend of mine and fellow dog owner told me that the first few months would be the hardest while you adapt and you think what the heck have I done? I was grateful for that advice as it prepared me for when those doubting thoughts popped up although she did tell me that it would pass quickly and in no time we would fall in love and it would be the best thing ever. This, I have to say, is spot on. We all adore her, even the stroppy teen does that should walk her more than he does but, of course, work and his virtual friends on his console get in the way. He walked her for ten minutes and forty-nine seconds tonight as I jokingly replied to his question of how long to walk her. I kid you not. His girlfriend is lucky, she gets attention but, then again, she is a lovely girl and he knows he is a lucky guy but would never admit it. We do see him interacting at times and kicking the football in a cool way so as not to act as if he cares too much.

Hannah loves her to bits. Before Jessie came along it was a fight to get her to walk to the car; nowadays she can walk for ages with Jessie and no complaints as she doesn't see walking the dog as a chore and enjoys the fun of taking control of the lead and having the responsibility of her dog. She calls her 'her sister' (but I don't know what Freud would glean from that!)

I have had friends that have lost their dogs in the last year prior to us having Jessie and, even though I had empathy for their loss, I didn't really understand it having never had a pet. I so get it now and have also become a fan of vet shows and admit to having shed a tear when an episode has shown a death of a pet as I can now relate to it. This was the part of getting a dog that I worried about. What if something happened and how would Hannah cope? I feel now, however, that the actual experience of having a pet, looking after them, etc, and, when the time comes, dealing with her loss (obviously this will not be for a very, very long time) will indeed help us all learn that this is the cycle of life and pets are included.

For now though, that is indeed a distant worry, one we will not dwell on, that we will put away or I will start blubbing at the thought. I will continue to enjoy being greeted by this wee, cheeky teddy bear face in the morning and love that she excitedly trots beside me happily and follows me about from room to room. I am even getting used to the licking that grossed me out to begin with, although not in Hannah's league; she is totally unfazed but I still retreat quickly (perhaps that's the nurse in me thinking of germs, etc).

I guess it's the unconditional love that I find endearing from dogs. I also always have that story stuck in my head that says dogs are loyal and if their owners died they would sit and pine for them whereas a cat would get over it and probably eat their owner for food – eek. Now, please don't ask me where I heard this but I did and, yes, it has always made me wary of cats (sorry cat lovers, I do agree that some are cute but crafty). Maybe this is why I kind of believe this story to be true although I am sure it is an old wives' tale, right?

I am proud to say that I have become a mad doggy mammy and I like it. Yes, it is hard work and the poop still smells bad and is 'eugh' to poop and scoop but that's what you've got to do. The benefits of having a dog in your house are lovely; it also gets you out and about more. We walk more as a family with the dog and there is nothing more lovely than her snuggling up close to you on the sofa. Yes, I know this is bad and that doggy school tells you not to. I think sometimes rules are made to be broken and this is one I let slide. She doesn't sit there all the time and, sure, pet therapy is known to help relieve stress and anxiety, so really it's for medicinal purposes.

Since her arrival I have lost the handle to my lovely wicker basket that she chewed, my mobile phone has been given a stamp of chewing, the lovely Dylon has had his post eaten, the hubby had a boot chewed and my wall got a chunk out of it during teething. I have had to puppy proof the house, put metal cornicing to stop chewing on the wall, put all footwear up out of reach, our garden has had new fencing to keep her safely in and finally, my sofa has been christened. She has had her first and last heat and will be getting spayed soon. It's only been nine months... Who knows what adventures she will bring in the next nine years?

If you are deciding on a dog for your family think hard on the decision. I look on it as a new member of the family that is here to stay. They are hard work but bring so much joy. They need walks and as we both work we have had to adapt our working days. I now walk her on my lunch break and the lovely Granny Ann dog sits after school with Hannah so she is not alone at home for more than a few hours. My parents were not so sure when we first got her but we know they love her to bits now, even Granda Harry who would pretend otherwise. A puppy really isn't just for Christmas but we are so looking forward to having her here with us for Christmas and many more, although I don't know how our love for real Christmas trees will fair this year with Jessie to contend with. Yes, we will be leaving a doggy stocking out for her too as she's worth it. Tiny paw prints, I'm sure, leave their mark on owners' hearts and we love having her wee paws entwined around our fingers. The Henrys are happy to welcome Jessie on board.

Just as I finish typing this, again, I hear the bellowing voice of my beloved shouting about having to clean our precious dog's bottom that had a bit of poop hanging off it. Yes, I giggled as I finished this, as I know he loves her really. Yes, those are your jobs: bins and the dog's private bits maintenance I thought to myself and remember, dear, you said, 'Let's get a dog, it will be fun'.

Prague and its Healing Powers

Now that we have gained a furry member to our family a wee break away on our own is even more important for our sanity. I am happy to report that Jessie is settling in well and is a valid and much loved member of the Henry household. From my writing it is evident we love a city break and this did pose a question of what to do with our beloved furry friend when we were away. Luckily, we have great comrades in Granny Ann and Auntie Laura who, between them, both looked after Hannah and Jessie. Apart from a minor disaster when Jessie ate into the box of hubby's cholesterol tablets that had been posted through the door, on the one hand she did well in the company of my family. My sister, on the other hand, was slightly traumatised at being greeted by a box of scattered tablets and poop when she arrived home. A quick count of tablets left and a search on Google showed that all would be well with the dog. She said it was a good job she was cute so she couldn't stay mad at her for long.

City breaks, I believe, are good for the soul and your relationship whether you are single, married or indeed a parent, but leaving the kids behind is the key. I believe they are vital to your mental health and they are a time when you can spend precious hours letting whatever city you visit embrace you and engage with your partner. You can leave behind the stress of work, families and, in our case, a demanding but adorable six-year-old and a teenage stepson. The latter has thrown us a trying time of late but I am sure that with tough love it will work itself out, even if it becomes a long and winding road instead of the scenic one we all wish for as parents. Parents sometimes beat themselves up too much if their parenting fails. I believe that, really, no matter how hard you try sometimes we have to step back and let our teenager think they know it all but knows nothing until they step into the real world, let's go of the reins and learns how the real world works if that's what they wish, warts and all.

On discussing my upcoming break with friends I had mixed reviews on their views of breaks alone, especially if one had kids. I was surprised that some, since becoming parents, have never had a break without their kids and there are others, like me, that live for these wee breaks to get back a bit of their self without their kids tagging along. I pondered on which kind of parent was the better parent, if any, and I concluded that neither was the better parent – we just parented differently. Just because some have never holidayed alone did not make me feel bad for doing so but it did make me think they were a little mad for not, ha! I get that a lot of it is to do with not having family nearby or someone to look after their kids although I also respected that some just felt they no longer wanted to do it at the moment and preferred all their holidays to include kids.

Again, I know we are very lucky that we have a great family support that they can babysit for short periods so we can escape. The one rule being that it is within the school week so that Granny Ann has the school day to break up the day for Hannah. This is fine for us as, with our shift work, we have weeks that we are off during the week so it's a win-win for all. We also keep Hannah amused by our daily video phone calls where she gets a wee look at whatever city we are in, a tour of our hotel room and a 'gleek' at our foods from different cultures. This also amuses our fellow restaurant guest who we see secretly smirk while pretending not to listen to the mad Irish couple blowing kisses and chatting enthusiastically to our cheeky six-year-old via the beauty of technology.

This time we decided to visit Prague. We agreed, instead of expensive Christmas presents, we would book a minibreak – much more enjoyable. Firstly, it didn't stop Mr Henry leaving a pair of dodgy-looking and paid-too-much-for earrings under the tree. He saw immediately from my face that I was bemused by the gift (my poker face is pathetic!) And they were dangly granny types at that! Secondly, the fact that he stated the shop assistant said they were a great pick (umm… because she was trying to make a sale, you silly man).

I have a friend whom we really should pay tribute to as our travel guide as we have followed her travel plans a lot in the past as she is so good (you know who you are, 'Summerbay'!) Her reviews and those of other friends made us decide on this destination. The nerd in me was ignited then and I researched weather updates, clothing requirements and hotels within walking distance of all attractions. In the space of a few weeks we had booked the trip, I had purchased my thermal gloves, Dr Martens walking boots that would be compatible with the cobblestone terrain (bargain in the half-price sale) and would also keep my tootsies warm.

We arrived at the airport check-in and I trundled beside Law while he navigated the long aisles of the airport with expertise, worked out our gate from the mad boards displayed and then pinpointed the nearest bar. I love this bit of your break when you are past security and you are seated beside the gate so you know you won't miss the flight. You then have that first sip of alcoholic beverage. Even though you are surrounded by TV daytime programmes, it doesn't matter as you're on holiday and allowed. You have no work commitments, the car is parked up in the long-stay car park and the kids are looked after. You can chill, let the cool beer settle your bones and get ready to relax and re-charge for a few days.

On our first day in Prague we settled into the hotel room which was lovely, central and really warm; actually really, really warm, that we were relieved when we found the button to regulate the heat or we would have been hanging out the windows for air. This was another talking point – the windows. Usually in our country, or maybe just from our hospital settings, you can never open windows very far. This hotel had gorgeous sash windows that opened fully so you could easily climb onto the ledge if you wanted to. Perhaps, as we have backgrounds in mental health nursing, this made us think this was a risk factor, but then we thought this also showed that this country has a better suicide rate than others, so we closed the windows with a little more ease. We just enjoyed the breeze without dwelling on the latter thought. Once a mental health nurse, always a mental health nurse!

That evening we had booked to do a beer tour of the city. We thought this would help us get a feel for the city and its geography. Well, actually, I thought of this for my hubby as my geography gene is shocking and I rely solely on Mr Henry's navigation skills on these trips. I happily trundle along beside him usually slightly inebriated, enveloping the culture of wherever we are. This seems to work for us, so why change it?

The tour was great 'craic' and just what we needed to kick back and relax. The tour guide was a fabulous young American 'Joey' who told us the history of the beer and bars we attended with enthusiasm and speed so we were captivated and not bored with the theory bit. We visited three lovely pubs and ate at the last one. The group was a mix of people from all over the globe and, after doing a wee scoot round the table to introduce ourselves, it kind of resembled an MDT meeting (for those not in the medical know it means a multidisciplinary meeting. We also probably came up with more solutions to many a problem that night than a normal ward meeting outcome, ha!)

There was a nice mixture of people; we had two lovely ladies from London who were physiotherapists, a doctor from Brazil, a lovely young couple from The Netherlands, a young eighteen-year-old from Brazil on a gap year, a data analyst from Austria who had lovely hair, plus us two Irish nurses. It was hilarious how our memories of being introduced to alcohol were much the same even though we were from different parts of the world. We were all guilty of having sneaked vodka from our parents' bottles as teenagers and diluting it with water so they wouldn't notice – we all had a giggle at that. I re-told the story of how I did this so well and sealed the bottle with such expertise that my dad, when offering a drink to his friend, was teased for being tight with his measures. After a few glasses he described how they felt no effect and how, on inspection, they had come to the conclusion that the bottle was pure water and so my mum had returned the bottle to the off-licence stating they had been sold a dud bottle – eek. Sorry Mammy and

Daddy but, yes, we did chuckle with the fear of being caught out and of the spectacle of Mammy returning the bottle with no doubt that we would have interfered with it and that it was wholly the fault of the distributors.

I was both in awe and fear at how young people travel so freely around the globe at a young age and I do admit that I asked the lovely gap year guy 'How does your mammy feel of you travelling on your own?' (Such an Irish mammy thing to do, I know!) I realise that I travelled to America on my own but I was in early twenties and clung to the group of friends I met at the start. I was even afraid to travel on the bus to my initial destination to meet people I knew would be there. I do see that with technology and video calls it is a lot better for parents to keep in touch nowadays, unlike my trip where it was payphones and writing letters that my parents relied on (I now get why my dad says I caused him to go bald with worry when growing up). Even now we have decided that if Hannah wants to travel so young we will let her, but secretly we will be in disguise at the back of the plane following her. I also learned that a lot of young people from America choose to come here to go to university as it is a third of the price and they also get to embrace a new culture while studying.

On our second day in Prague we enjoyed gorgeous food in proper Czech cuisine restaurants. They were such good value and hearty. We learned from our beer tour that Czechs do not have a lot of vegetables in their diet. Really, apart from perhaps a few chillies or peppers it really is quite protein charged and filled with dumplings or bread – but very delicious. We tried pork knees, goulash and buffalo medallions – all yum. A tip for anyone visiting is to stay away from the main square area as it is quite pricey, but if you meander down the side streets you will fall into great wee places that have delicious food at better prices. This also applies to the beer in the main square. Beer is sold at similar prices to home but, again, down the side streets the beer prices drop to around one to two euros per pint.

We had a funny experience in a very traditional Czech pub we visited. On falling in quite merry from the freedom that holidays bring, coupled with the glow from a few beers we had consumed, we faced a very angry looking barman. Law asked for two beers and was met with a furious, gesticulating man pointing to different beers – eek. I decided to retreat to the bathroom and leave Law to it. The bathroom was a small lean-to at the entrance of the bar. As I exited after use I never gave a thought whether the door had closed properly, assuming like most pub doors they automatically shut after you. I had not sat down properly when the barman, again, began gesticulating madly to the barmaid and then I realised the toilet door was slightly ajar. He slammed the door shut and I shouted an apology, which is when he shouted back, 'It's OK', but in a way that did not emulate he was OK about it. Law and I quietly giggled and awaited our beers, praying they would not be thrown over our heads. He arrived at our table and banged the beers down followed by our change that he practically threw across the table. Now, at this stage we were transfixed by his manner both in amusement and fear – eek.

Shortly after, two girls entered the pub and I watched open-mouthed as the door also didn't shut properly after they had entered. My inner voice screeched Nooooooo... but it was too late, the barman had seen. He again began gesticulating madly with his arms at the two confused girls. They immediately shut the door tight and went to sit, but he again began motioning madly in a shooing manner. The girls, again confused, asked if he was closing up. He nodded enthusiastically and shooed again. The girls scurried out the door and we looked on in amusement and fear once more. Law observed that perhaps he had had one too many beers and had no tolerance. I agreed that maybe he did look inebriated and forgot that he was running a pub and it was not his living-room that people had stumbled into. There were a few Americans seated at the table beside us so I asked them what they thought of the barman. They laughed and said that they had checked out the reviews and the first comment was that the barman was an 'ass****'. That made us all laugh and not feel it was only us that had caused his reaction. We did not order a second pint; we enjoyed living and wanted to continue our trip to attempt this.

Our second night ended in an Irish bar – you cannot travel and not visit an Irish bar – if you're Irish it's ingrained in us all. Here we enjoyed more beers with lots of friendly bar staff. There was a lovely Czech girl, Sally, who was a credit to the bar, so friendly, and worked that bar with such speed it was as if we had pushed a fast-forward button. No sooner had we ordered our beers that we looked up and they had arrived. There was a great band on and as the drink went down we wound down and Bendy Wendy appeared (Bendy Wendy is me when the effects of alcohol hit; my limbs move but not always in co-ordination).

The next thing I know my hubby has me on the dance floor doing his daddy dancing, but in his head he is John Travolta... We are quickly joined by another couple and all four of us swing our limbs wildly that it could have been portrayed that we may require medical assistance, only that our laughs and animated faces reassured the other revellers all was good – we were just crazy dancers.

After this we sat in the other couple's company and chatted freely, learning they were Czech and German. We loved hearing their stories about how much the Czech people had gained from the fall of communism. I have to admit, I only knew slices of information but I did research the next day and am happy that this generation of people have so much more opportunities and live in less oppressive ways now. They asked us to come dancing with them at the local nightclub. Even though it was way past our bedtime we embraced their hospitality and, in seconds, we were whisked from the bar and found ourselves dancing in an abandoned manner once again on a dance floor that was manned by a robot DJ – yep, a robot! My hubby, in his euphoric state, thought it would be fun to record our antics. I, in my inebriated state, didn't care and so we danced like no one was watching (except they were and the entire Internet, thanks to the new 'live' button). It wasn't until the next day that this became apparent and oh, how I cringed and laughed when we saw the evidence and the comments on our dancing. I finally dragged my hubby out of the club at 3.30am as, after thinking it would finish soon, I suddenly realised it was going to go on all night. On the one hand, my body at that stage was shutting down; my moves were getting dodgier and unsafe as one leg at a time was going to sleep having given up on the rest of my body joining in. I observed that Mr Henry, on the other hand, had a few good hours left of his dodgy moves, but as I needed him as navigator to walk home he had to come with me. We bid farewell to the lovely couple, thanked them for their hospitality and stumbled the short walk home in a giddy mood, laughing at our moves and the fact that I had gone clubbing in a checked shirt dress and DM boots. This is another plus of visiting cities as you don't care about these things and you just live for the moment and go with the flow.

On our last day we wandered the streets of Prague, took in the beauty of Charles Bridge and how pretty it was as night fell with the old-style lamps lighting it so majestically against the water. We wandered around the Jewish quarter, visited the old Jewish Cemetery, a deceptively haunting and beautiful place all at the same time. I was moved learning about the Terezín concentration camp. I was so moved when viewing the children's gallery of paintings they had drawn whilst there. I learned that these drawings occurred at art classes, that one of the ladies, Friedl Dicker-Brandeis, had adopted them during her studies at Bauhaus before being interned here. Really, she used art as a tool to help the kids try and channel the madness of that time. It was art therapy and in some of the pictures the kids filled their pages with drawings of soldiers and the fear that they felt. You also could see how they were encouraged to ignite hope by drawing pictures depicting how they saw life would be outside the gate and their dreams of returning home. You could not view these paintings without being choked and, no matter if you were a mammy or not, your heart felt sore when you thought of the children and what they had to endure. How, even now in this day and age, with the madness going around the world with Syria and other countries, that it is the children that are the innocent victims but yet, even as I felt sad about this, I also had hope in me that the world will get better. I guess if we give up on hope then we have nothing.

Before this lady was transferred to Auschwitz she had filled two suitcases with roughly 4,500 children's drawings and hid them. After the war they were found and handed over to the Jewish Museum. After learning that only a few of these children survived as most were sent to Auschwitz and met their death, it made me feel that doing what Friedl did, she in effect commemorated those children's lives. By hiding these drawings, which are now displayed, it shows that their lives mattered; they live on and we learn from seeing them and acknowledge their existence. I left that place saying a silent prayer and feeling very blessed for what I have.

As mentioned earlier, when we got married I walked down the aisle to Pachelbel's Canon, a piece of music that has stuck in my head from my school days after a good friend played it so beautifully on her flute. While in Prague I spied a poster for Vivaldi: The Four Seasons concert and convinced my hubby to go. He admitted classical music was not his cup of tea but would go for the love of his woman and probably more for the promise of lots of beer after it, ha. Now, I am not a big fan of classical music myself but love some pieces and this was a very upbeat performance with pieces that, even if you did not know the name, you would definitely have recognised. I loved it, especially Pachelbel's Canon and the acoustics were amazing even though the cathedral was colder than outside and yes, the husband was rewarded for sitting through it with me with lots of beer after.

Would I recommend Prague to anyone? Indeed I would, it is definitely good for the soul. It is pretty and powerful in teaching you about history and its culture through music and historic buildings. It also brings you peace of mind, helps to clear the head and unwind while you are wandering around. A must is the beer tour to just emerge in the history and knowledge of beer with tasting involved. It also gives you a chance to meet lots of different people from all parts of the world – that adds to the fun of the night. We were lucky that we had a great group that gelled quickly and I have never laughed so much with a group of strangers, so good for the soul. We also think they coped very well with our accent and likewise us with the language barrier at times. It didn't really seem to cause problems even as the drink went in.

City breaks I definitely think are a great practice whether you're single, married and definitely as parents. Why? Well, it makes you remember what you like about your spouse when you take away the stresses of work, life and kids (that, as I've said, you have to admit can make you have bad thoughts about your other half a lot!) You just concentrate on you and enjoy the freedom that holidays bring: daytime drinking, soaking up the culture, etc. We only live once and the world is a big place so to not attempt to visit outside our own doorstep would be a shame. Our Austrian friend from the beer tour commented on this using the expression YOLO and this is so true. We will continue to explore the beauty of this world we live in with Hannah and on city breaks alone. We may be more aware of not using the 'live' button on the Internet next time or perhaps not as why shouldn't we share our fun? If you don't like, you don't have to watch!

HUMOUR IS THE CAPE THAT HELPS GUIDE US THROUGH LIFE'S MINEFIELDS

I have said before through many of these stories that humour has got me through many a minefield not only in general but also in 'Mammyville'. I am sure most of the population would agree that in the worst of times it has pulled us through and picked us up when we thought we never would. Perhaps being Irish means that this humour is ingrained as part of our culture. This got me thinking that maybe that is how we are made so that not only when something extremely funny occurs it makes us laugh but that it is also activated in those awkward and 'total despair' moments just so we can catch a breath, re-group, regain strength and get on with the madness that is life in all its glory.

I have had many an awkward moment even before 'Mammyville' where humour has indeed been my saviour. Opening my memory vault to write this has made me giggle so much tonight already that I needed that injection of laughter. Would I be the only one that has ever walked down the street and banged into a lamppost when I had turned to look the other way and lost my bearings? I have also been the gal that has caused someone to do the same. Once I was pumping petrol (yes, one time I did remember to fill up on time!) and spied my aunt out walking, so I shouted, 'Hello' and, as she turned and waved, she walked into a lamppost – eek. Was it wrong that even though I knew it must have hurt her I couldn't help but chuckle as it was funny? Sorry Auntie Gretta.

Interviews can also cause those awkward moments. My first interview with an agency after university was indeed awkward. Halfway through it I swung my leg a little too much in nervousness and lost my shoe. For the rest of the interview I attempted to retrieve the same under the table with my foot. When this was not working I contemplated leaving quickly, one shoe less, and hoping they wouldn't notice. Once the interview was over, which had gone well despite my inner turmoil, I was faced with what to do about my shoe. My brain was on fire – one thought was saying Leave shoe and exit quickly and the other thought was screaming Retrieve your shoe, you mad woman! What did I choose? I chose the mad woman thought. I thanked the interviewers, shook their hands and excused myself as I retrieved my shoe from under the table. I replaced it confidently and exited the room without looking back. I am sure I heard sniggers but they must have been impressed by my recovery as I was offered a job. Did I laugh out loud later when re-telling the story to friends? Of course I did but at the time I wished for the superpower of becoming invisible. Since then I have had a recent interview that tops them all. All will be revealed in the second book – ha.

I was the girl in university who, after suffering from insomnia, a visit to the doctor told me to exercise more and this would help me to sleep. That day on my way to catch the bus I spied a sale of small trampolines in a shop window and in my mind saw that as a sign. I headed to the till and awaited my small trampoline. What was dispatched was a huge, flat, square box nearly the size of me with a picture of a trampoline emblazoned on it. What did I do? Others around me sniggered at my purchase and watched as to how I would react. What I did was confidently take hold of the box under my arm and drag it out of the shop with an air of 'Hell, I knew it was going to be this size' attitude. I dragged it on the bus much to the amusement of the driver and passengers and dragged it off at my stop, head held high, again ignoring the sniggers. Thank the Lord my student house was only around the corner and, when my housemate opened the door to me and I explained my purchase, we spent the next ten minutes laughing uncontrollably. The ironic thing is that this was supposed to help aid my sleep but it only served to interrupt it more as when my housemates and I headed home after the pub on many a night we thought it was great 'craic' to jump on it while eating our kebabs, dance on it to loud music and hence keep everyone up in the house that was trying to sleep. It did bring us many a laugh though and fun memories, so a good purchase all round.

In my work I have made many faux pas, but the one that still makes me laugh to myself is a few years ago. In a ward round I confidently told the whole team that I had informed the paramilitaries (!) that a patient had MRSA (I was meant to say 'paramedics'! Yup, a Freudian slip from an Irish nurse, maybe). It did make the team laugh a lot and more so when I realised what I had said. What could I do but join in at the same time? I wished the ground would swallow me up.

When I worked a summer in America I accidently let two iguanas out of their cages while doing a chambermaid shift. Imagine the fear when maring the bed when I see these two baby lizard things jumping all around the room after knocking the cage over. In my fear and nervousness I laughed as I grabbed bundles of the guests 'clothes and threw them over the reptiles. I continued to manically laugh as I went in search of my fellow Irish travelling companions for help who were also working there. The three of us, through tears of laughter, managed to return the creatures to their cages and tidy the room, all before the guests returned – and we didn't get sacked. Oh, how we laughed from relief after that episode…

Since becoming a mammy I think in those early weeks when you are tired, humour is a tool you cling onto for dear life. This gorgeous bundle that you have prayed hard for arrives and then they cause mayhem. Yes, it may be mostly good mayhem – laughter, gurgles and baby smiles, but it is also a double-edged sword of sleep deprivation, bloodcurdling squeals where you and your other half sometimes stand half asleep at 'stupid o'clock' in the morning, passing the child from one to another thinking What the heck is wrong with this crazy child? Does anyone agree? In those moments you laugh as if you didn't, you would go off your head and run for the hills. I remember one morning after a no sleep kind of night (due to teething monsters) I made a dash to the chemist as I could not see properly at home and was too tired to search our cupboard myself. I went straight to the counter and asked for 'a tube of Bonjela, please'. I then noticed the confused and smirking face of the cashier and then my peripheral vision kicked in before she spoke. I could see wine, vodka and cigarettes on the shelf. Yup, I had headed into the off-licence that was next door to the chemist. The cashier laughed as she confirmed my madness and then she said that perhaps my brain is telling me to get wine as well and then we laughed before I sheepishly left the building like the mad mammy I had become.

Travelling by car with a crying child is also a time when mad mammies would do anything to silence the madness. My Hannah, when she was a baby, seemed to love us mooing like cows, which would send her into fits of giggles (each to their own). Now, imagine a hot day and I have the window down while driving. Hannah begins to cry, I am approaching a roundabout and so I can't pull over. I do what I know will work, I start mooing like a cow while looking at her through the rear-view mirror and it works. Pleased with myself, I turn to my right and come face to face with the man in the car next to me who is staring at me in disbelief with his mouth hanging open. He obviously didn't know why I was mooing like a crazy thing and as the traffic began to move I couldn't explain. I laughed all the way home as I kept seeing his confused face in my head and I am sure that made other drivers think I had completely lost the plot but, hey, my baby was silent and I was full of endorphins, so a win-win really, right? I have also let my husband head out to the pub with his mates knowing full well that our baby Hannah had spewed a lovely trail right down the back of his black top when he gave her a cuddle before he left, just because it made me laugh out loud for ages after he left. I know... but I was very tired that night and not feeling myself.

As I keep mentioning that laughter is my tonic, I shall tell you of another story. Even at the saddest times in my life I can remember how laughter saved me. One was when I was hospitalised trying to keep Jacob's labour from progressing. I re-call losing my courage and having a meltdown; I was walking around the room in pain and begging Lawrence not to let me go mad. He, of course, was being supportive and then I caught a glimpse of my tear-stained, wide-eyed and scared face in the mirror, my wild hair like I had been electrocuted. I turned to him and said 'Sack that thought, I am already there'. He then looked at me as if not knowing what to say and we burst out laughing. We laughed so hard for ten minutes and that gave us time to breathe and get back on track in what was the saddest chapter in our lives. It kept us sane in that moment.

Funerals are also always times when I have often thought that maybe someone up above attempts to lighten the mode by injecting humorous moments. When we lost our Granny Harkin we were all heartbroken. She lived with us at the weekend for years and so we had a deep bond. At the mass my younger sister began to cry and I moved closer to her to offer comfort. At that moment she looked up and her eyelashes were covered in pieces of tissue that she looked as if she had been caught in a snowstorm. Oh, how I laughed as silently as I could as we were in a chapel. When my lovely mother-in-law passed away it was heartbreaking and, as she was leaving the house to go to the chapel, I was stood next to my sister-in-law, Christine. Everyone was sad and numb with grief and as the coffin took off, being carried by her family, a bird decided to poop and my sister-in-law and I watched as the trousers of my husband and the other pall-bearers got a few drops of the poop on landing. I remember in a day of such sadness that for those few seconds when we both linked arms with each other and couldn't help but giggle which, for a brief second, let us breathe and escape the reality of that day that was difficult to comprehend.

Car journeys are another minefield where humour saves the day. If I mention IKEA in our family we all have a nervous laugh after our girly trip turned into a nightmare. We got lost on the way there but when we finally arrived, shopped and were purchasing our items we had a fit of giggles at the cash desk when I was asked for my loyalty card. I told the wide-eyed teenager that IKEA had near broken our family getting here and we had no loyalty towards it now. When we realised the critter had no clue what we were on about we all burst into laughter, proper belly laughs that you have no control over. The poor guy was glad to see us leave. We then had a job getting my sister's mirror in the car which meant Granny Ann had to sit like she was carrying a cross all the way home as the mirror went the whole length of the car and rested on her shoulder. We finally got home 3hrs later after having to be escorted onto the motorway twice by two taxi men, having previously missed the turn-off to Derry twice! As I've said, my sense of direction is not my best asset. Hannah, who was three at the time, found it all hilarious. She still talks about the trip and says we were all shouting and that she had to pee at the side of the road. Yup, that trip was not a warm and fuzzy trip but, yet again, humour helped us through.

To end my debut book of stories (I have still many more for the second book if this goes well – ha) of 'Mammyville' and all its madness I think that the humour button is alive and well in all of us and probably was designed to help us through the mad, sad, happy and downright confusing episodes in this world we live in – especially when you enter the mammy chapter. I think that if you let go of this tool then you can enter a very dark place. I urge you all, especially mad mammies, to hold onto that cape and let it guide you through the minefields, embrace the fun times and gain comfort in sad times. Life is hard and sometimes we need to allow our emotions out no matter the occasion. Laughter really is the best medicine. When you think about it, after you have really laughed, no matter what the occasion, you have to admit you feel better, stronger and ready to face the world. Now, go hit your funny bone and laugh not! That really is not funny, right? But ironic, eh?

Printed in Great Britain
by Amazon

67230266R00116